LEGEND

1620	Moses Fletcher	*Mayflower*
	Falmouth to Plymouth	
1630	Robert Fletcher	
	Falmouth to Concord, MA	
1641	John Heald	
	Liverpool to Concord, MA	
1703	Samuel Heald	
	Liverpool to PA	

GENEALOGY OF A REBEL:

An Autobiography and Documentary

BY

E. MAXINE EDWARDS

ISBN 0-9668779-0-X

Library of Congress Catalog Card Number: 98-94946

Printed by
Maverick Publications
P.O. Box 5007
Bend, Oregon 97708

DEDICATED TO

O.C. Wood

ACKNOWLEDGEMENTS

Special thanks to Shelley Green, Weed branch librarian; College of the Siskiyous library staff; ILL Librarian, Kathy Fuston, Yreka; Family History Center volunteers, Mt. Shasta Church of Jesus Christ of Latter Day Saints; Mrs. Eka Parkinson; relatives Jack Heald, President of the Heald Genealogical Society; Robert M. Wood; Oren Wood; Dale M. Caragata; Fay Wood; Lucille Palmer; Connie Clark; Norma Whitbread; and to all my friends and family who have endured my "obsession" with digging up my roots.

TABLE OF CONTENTS

CHAPTER 1

"At my nativity
The front of heaven was full of fiery shapes
of burning cressets; and at my birth
The frame and huge foundation of the earth
Shak'd like a coward."

King Henry IV, Act III, Scene I
William Shakespeare

Unlike the meteorological pyrotechnics which welcomed the mighty Glendower, the heavens wept when I was born[1] but other signs were more auspicious. My arrival coincided with All Saints' Day, 1919, a year that epitomized the spirit of social change sweeping America, *i.e.* Woman Suffrage, Prohibition, and the adjustment to peace following World War I.

According to the ephemeris, people born under my astrological sign (Scorpio, a water sign) "are sensual, sensitive, and psychic," while *Mother Goose* predicts that Saturday's child works hard for its living. For the pure quill of prognostication, I can vouch for Mother Goose.

The records show that I was born in the Multnomah County Hospital in Portland, Oregon. Being born in a hospital was not that common seventy-seven years ago when most of America was still rural and most self-respecting babies were born at home. Because custom demanded a ten-day confinement, my mother and I probably spent the first ten days of my life in the hospital.

After that, almost three years elapsed before the episode occurred which is my first memory. As I recall, I was standing on the porch of a shingled bungalow built up on stilts and listening to the loud voices cursing and screaming inside. Then the door bursts open and a man in uniform comes out. He picks me up, tosses me up in the air, and says, "You're the only one I'll miss." Then he puts me down and trips down the steps to the road and marches out of my life forever. I never saw my father again.

Following that traumatic episode, I was relocated to a one-room apartment in down-town Oakland, California, in the custody of my maternal grandmother, Laura Anna Heald.[2] The room was about ten by twelve square feet, containing a single cot, a straight chair, built-in cupboards across one end, with counter top, sink, and single burner hot plate. Since the cot was too narrow for both of us, I slept on the floor with a coat or rug over me. The communal bathroom was down the hall to the rear of the building, so the hall door was left unlocked. In the apartment, the amenities were limited to a calendar hanging on the wall beside the door and a *Love Story* magazine. With my grandmother gone all day, I had plenty of time to learn to read. The calendar provided a visual representation of the names of the days of the week and months of the year which I had memorized. Using these visual symbols as a basis for comparison, it was obvious that January and February both ended in *ary* and had the same sound /ăr-ĕ/, so it seemed reasonable to conclude that that combination of letters represented a linguistic constant. Likewise, the *ember* in September, November, and December, the *Ju* in June and July, and *day* in the days of the week, reinforced this hypothesis. By extrapolation, it seemed logical to assume that all of the syllables in the names of the days and months had a constant value. By matching known syllables with the printed text in the magazine, I was soon decoding new words, and aided by pictures and context, learning to read.

When I heard the newspaper boy yelling, "EXTRA! EXTRA! Read all about it!" I would climb up on the chair under the window, which opened on an alley, and crane my neck to see the big black print at the top of the paper. In this manner, I was able to add two more syllables to my decoding repertory.

While language is learned aurally, learning to read requires the synergy of sight and sound: visual symbols (letters) in sync with phonics. Phonics without visual representation would be no more efficacious to the decoding process than a recording of farm-yard sounds. Therefore, the emphasis on "phonics" alone as the key to learning to read is inherently misleading at best.

Although I was not supposed to leave the room except to use the restroom, sometimes I would go out on the loggia, which was about six feet above street level, and watch the people hurrying by, without being noticed myself. But one day I was noticed. An old man wearing a black suit, black top hat, and a long white beard stopped at the base of the stone steps leading up to the loggia. He was carrying a red harp. He looked up at me and asked if I would like to have it. Naturally I said that I would, so he hobbled up the steps and handed the harp to me and left. I lugged the instrument to our room and just sat there on the chair, hugging the harp. For the first time in my life, I owned something—something that was all mine. I was still sitting there when my grandmother came home. She asked who had given the harp to me. When I explained, she said that it had to be returned, so she took it and left.

One day my grandmother took me to what would probably be called Day Care today. There was a lady in charge of six or seven other children who were seated on kid-sized chairs at a low, round wooden table. But miracle of miracles, each child was clutching a slender cylinder of wood or colored wax which left a rainbow of colors on the scratch paper provided. Here was a whole new world of communication and artistic expression. Talk about Pig Heaven! The time flew and soon Grandmother was picking me up. When she inquired about my day, the lady told her not to bring me back; I didn't belong there. I should be in the third grade, not kindergarten. So much for Pig Heaven!

Another incident that I remember was being led down the hall by a man. He opened the door to a vacant room, took me inside, and closed the door. He unfastened his trousers, which dropped around his ankles. Then we heard footsteps in the hall. I turned to watch the door to see who else might be joining us, but the footsteps passed on by. I turned back to the man, but he was gone, obviously out the window to the alley. This strange behavior made me realize that something was wrong, and therefore to avoid similar situations in the future. Since I would not have gone anywhere with a stranger, the man had to be someone I knew, a family member or an acquaintance, as are most child molesters.

Nothing remarkable occurred after that until March 1924. My grandmother and I were in the back seat of a car and two men in the front. It was night and the rain was drumming on the roof of the vehicle as it sped along the highway. Through the isinglass windows of the car curtains, I could see the lamp posts flashing by. Then, suddenly, the car was in the ditch, lying on its side. Except for my black eye, no one was injured. My grandmother and I were transported to the Sacramento train depot by a good Samaritan. The waiting room at the railroad station had pew-like benches as well as chairs and a coat rack. Grandmother hung her coat on the rack and lay down on one of the benches. Then she started having chills, a nervous reaction to the accident. She told me to bring her coat. I climbed up on a chair and was trying to unhook the heavy garment, when I heard the street door open.

CHAPTER 2

"There is a tide in the affairs of men,
which, taken at the flood, leads to fortune."

Julius Caesar, Act IV, Scene III
William Shakespeare

The newcomer was a middle-aged, well-dressed, overweight woman with a coyote fur boa around her neck and a doctor's black instrument bag in her hand. She saw my dilemma and came to my rescue. She covered my grandmother with the coat and listened to her report of the accident. Then she sat down on a chair, opened the black bag, and began munching on its contents. Until then, my diet had been primarily Post Toasties and tea, so I didn't recognize roast duck, potato salad, deviled eggs, cookies, and other goodies which she proceeded to devour. Misunderstanding my avid curiosity, she offered me a piece of the duck. I looked at Grandmother for permission before accepting the dark meat. I didn't find it particularly palatable, but then roast duck is probably an acquired taste. The salad was easier to chew and, therefore, less painful to my bad teeth. The eggs were soft, the cookies hard.

Having appeased her appetite for the moment, the woman introduced herself as Mattie Wood. She lived on a ranch in northern Nevada but was on her way to Chico, where her mother was dying. Later in the conversation, she idly remarked that she would like to have a little girl like me. Imagine her consternation when Grandmother said, "Take her."

The first place that my new mother took me was to a barber shop and ordered a Dutch bob. The barber placed a board across the arms of the barber chair so that my head was above the chair back and started cutting. Things went smoothly until he turned on the electric clippers, which sounded like a combine, burned my neck, and pulled out as much hair as they cut. It only took four adults to hold me still enough to complete the operation.

When the Western Pacific train pulled out of the station heading north, my foster mother and I were on it. Seated beside the window, I soon tired of watching the flat lands of the Central valley flash by, so I turned my attention to the upholstery on the seat and the wooden arm rests at each end. This observation led to a visual comparison of the width of the seat and height of the back. They appeared the same, but I had no way to measure the actual dimensions, until I realized that the top of my head was even with the top of the seat back and my feet were flush with the edge of the seat. Therefore, a reversal of my position, putting my back on the seat and my legs against the back rest, should prove or disprove my estimation. No sooner thought than done. My head and feet were even with the edges of the seat and back. Exactly the same! But my triumph was short lived. Mother grabbed me and hustled me down the aisle to the restroom at the end of the passenger car where she told me how much my unlady-like behavior had humiliated and embarrassed her and never to do it again.

Back in my seat, I sat like a graven image until we passed a sand hill crane posing on one leg on a levee. Instantly, I wondered if I could do that, but a glance at Mother's forbidding expression warned me to postpone that experiment.

Fortunately, we arrived in Chico before I could get into any more trouble.

Unfortunately, no place is mischief proof. Banished to the backyard with the ducks because of "Grandma's" critical condition, complications of diabetes, I promptly got into hot water, or actually, duck water. Apparently I was observed drinking from the duck pan. While I don't recall doing it, I probably was guilty. After all, I was pretending to be a duck, following the principle that when in Rome, do as the Romans do, in this case ducks. The ducks didn't object, but Mother did, vociferously. This time she was mortified, as in vexed, chagrined, or humiliated, or all of the above. Granting the somberness of the situation, it still seemed an over-reaction. After all, I was the one who would suffer the consequences if the water was as contaminated as she believed. My immune system must have been working overtime because I never developed any of the predicted plagues.

On March 20, 1924, Grandma Flaugher died with dignity at the home of her son-in-law, A. A. Rogers, who operated a grocery store on Laurel Street.[3] After the funeral at the Westfall Chapel, Reverend H. M. Law officiating, Grandma was interred in the Chico Cemetery. Attending the services were her daughter, Mattie Wood, son, James Flaugher, sister, Mrs.

Martha Pierce of Madrid, Iowa, son-in-law, Aivy A. Rogers, and numerous friends.[4]

From Chico, Mother and I back-tracked (no pun intended) to Marysville, then northeast to Flanigan, the junction to the Nevada, California, Oregon railroad, facetiously referred to as the "narrow-crooked-and ornery,"[5] which carried us to Alturas, California. There we caught the Surprise Valley Stage over Cedar Pass to Cedarville.

Because of the deep snow, we continued our journey east to Nevada with horses and sleigh to Old Vya, one of the original trading posts on the emigrant trail to the '49 way station and points north and west. Although it was officially spring, the days were still short, and darkness had fallen by the time we reached Vya, so we spent the night there.

In 1924, Layton A. Mariette was proprietor of the post and his wife, Eva B., was postmaster.[6] They had two children, a six-year-old boy, Maxwell, and two-year-old girl, Mildred.

While Mrs. Mariette was preparing supper (dinner), she had to go down in the cellar to get something, leaving the trap door in the kitchen floor open. Maxwell seized the opportunity to try to push me into the hole. I managed to save myself by clutching Mother's skirts. Then he shoved me onto the stove, burning my elbow. This behavior is typical of a spoiled child whose parents indulged his every whim. Later Dad told me that he had once suggested to the boy that playing with the hammer and the clock was lots of fun. Needless to say, Dad was *persona non grata* for a long time afterward.

The next morning, we started the twenty-one mile trip to Mosquito Valley and home. The first order of business when traveling with live horse-power is to half-fill the wagon or sleigh with hay for the horses to eat at rest stops. It also provides soft seating for passengers. For emergencies, food, bedding, and fire-building materials like matches and kindling were always carried.

There was no sightseeing. The snow covered the fences and buried the few buildings along the way, but our team, a gray Percheron and a sorrel Belgian, needed no sign posts to find their way home, and a frozen crust on the snow allowed them to cross submerged fences and other obstacles without breaking through.

The first glimpse of my new home was a small black triangle, the house gable, peeking through the drifts. In front of our destination, mother and I waited in the sleigh while Dad unhooked the traces and led the horses to the bed of the vehicle to munch hay while he shoveled a passage to the kitchen door. Inside, he lighted the kerosene lamp and built fires in both cook stove and heater in the living room. The lamp was necessary because snow covered the windows leaving the interior as dark as night. Then he went out to lead the horses to the barn where they were unharnessed, fed, and watered. As soon as the livestock were attended to, Dad unloaded the supplies from the sleigh. In the meantime, I was introduced to my new home. On my right as I entered was a large wood box filled with aromatic red juniper, the Home Comfort range with oven below, water reservoir at one end and warming ovens above, a glass-fronted china cabinet, and a cot beside the wall. In the middle of the room was a large mahogany table with matching chairs. Along the rear wall were a White treadle sewing machine under the window, an armchair, and a rocking chair. On the left side of the room was a small table where the *Old Testament* held a pride of place when the table was not being used for writing letters, doing homework, or as a card table. Next to it was a doorway opening into the living room. Continuing counter-clockwise from the doorway were cupboards and counter space. Adjacent to the outside door was a sturdy shelf for water buckets, wash basin, and towel racks, with slop pail and clothes hamper below.

The living room was furnished with a pot-bellied wood heater, book cases, console model phonograph, easy chairs, and a large black bear-skin rug sans head and claws. Above the book case was a trophy deer head with forty-four points and a forty-four inch spread. It was my foster brother's first buck, killed by a lucky shot which cut its throat and wasted no meat. At eighteen, George was justly proud of his contribution to the family table. Game was hunted for food not sport. On the opposite wall was a freak rack of antlers, a forked horn that measured forty-two inches from the base to the tip and had had a forty-two inch spread. With its forked horns for insurance, the animal had lived to a ripe old age before it was finally killed.

There were doors in all four walls: one to the front porch, one to my bedroom, one to the master bedroom, and another to the kitchen-dining room. Beside the door to my room hung a framed copy of Kipling's poem *If*, the conditions of which I adopted for my own goals. If they were good enough for a man, they were good enough for me.

My bedroom had a white iron bedstead, chair, dresser with mirror, night stand with coal oil lamp on top, chamber pot inside, and a throw rug.

But more important, the door provided privacy, and tenancy entailed responsibility for keeping my new domain ship-shape.

The master bedroom was larger but similarly furnished. The extra space accommodated several large trunks: one of pictures, mainly snapshots; one of linens and handkerchiefs; one of silk floss, peacock feathers and ostrich plumes, and another of Indian artifacts. Mother's fine collection of hand-painted porcelain cups and saucers were on display in the china closet kitchen.

By the time that Dad had finished the chores outdoors, Mother had the evening meal ready and served in style: linen napery, china dinner-ware, silverware and cut glass sugar bowl, creamer, butter dish, vinegar cruet, and salt and pepper shakers with silver tops. By necessity pioneer diet relied heavily on meat and potatoes, home-made bread, dairy products, and eggs, all high cholesterol foods. To balance this heavy fare, Nature provided a variety of greens: lamb's quarter, mustard, and nettles; wild mushrooms which grew in our meadow; wild plums, choke-cherries, and service berries. Because of the short growing season, only hardy plants like rhubarb, gooseberries, and root crops were practical. Of course, nothing was wasted. Watermelon rinds became preserves, green tomatoes substituted for meat in mincemeat, and other unripened produce wound up in a pickle. As commendable as these culinary expedients were, I was less interested in food than in observing my new "father."

At fifty-one, his square face was weathered to a leathery brown and his clear brown eyes were buried in wrinkles caused by years of squinting against the sun, wind, dust, and snow. His chin was cleft, his mouth straight, and his dark brown hair fine as silk. But his most prominent feature was a large arched nose between high cheek bones. His likeness to Sitting Bull, Chief of the Sioux Nation, often aroused curiosity and speculation, but personal questions in the old West were taboo. In a political climate where the "only good Indian was a dead Indian," bragging about one's Indian heritage was hardly the healthiest way to make friends and influence people. As a child in the Dakotas, Dad had known Sitting Bull and even learned the Sioux war chant, but it was not Sioux blood that coursed in his veins. His paternal grandmother was an Oneida Mohawk, one of the five Iroquois Nations in New York,[7] and his maternal grandmother was Almira Aldridge (Aldrich),[8] one of an estimated two million descendants of Princess Pocahontas, the non-pariel of Virginia.[9]

But at that first meal together, ancestry was the least of my worries. I had no idea what I was eating, let alone how to eat it. By following Dad's example, I learned the proper dining ritual without asking questions. When he excused himself and carried his dishes to the counter, I did likewise. Then I tried to dry the dishes for Mother, but I was so short that I couldn't keep the dish towel off the floor, so she said that she would finish up.

When I entered the living room, Dad was already engrossed in a book. He looked up and handed me a book with pictures. To his surprise, I zeroed in on the text. He wasn't sure if I was reading or just pretending so he asked some pertinent questions. Having poor verbal skills due to my long isolation and lack of practice, I stumbled over some pronunciations but I responded intelligently. His face lit up. Being a self-educated person himself, he could relate to my thirst for knowledge.

An unfortunate accident had cut short his formal education in the seventh grade. One weekend, while he and his younger brother, Arden, were running around the barnyard, Dad stepped on a pitchfork, left lying on the ground. A tine penetrated his left boot and calf. Not unexpectedly, infection set in, followed by gangrene. When the doctor was called, he examined the mortification of the flesh and declared that Dad would die unless his leg was amputated. His mother said, "Then let him die. I already have one cripple." She was referring to her oldest son, Frank, who had had infantile paralysis when he was about three years old, leaving him paralyzed from the waist down. Since there was no room in the old West for weaklings, she immediately apprenticed him to his grandfather, Abram Faust, in Pennsylvania, who was a cobbler. There Frank could learn a trade that was not dependent on legs.

Obviously Dad did not die, but he was bedridden for almost a year before he recovered. That year was spent studying. He memorized the *Bible*; explored the teachings of the Greek philosophers, Socrates, Plato, and Aristotle; Agreed with Cato's condemnation of ostentation (conspicuous consumption); pondered the works of Hegel, Kant, and Marx; questioned Nietzsche's "perfectibility of man;" accepted Darwin's theory of evolution, Einstein's theory of relativity, and Mendel's Law of genetics. Before his accident, he had aspired to a legal career, so Robert Ingersoll and Clarence Darrow represented his ideal of American jurisprudence. In music, he favored the violin; in sports, the manly art of self-defense. But no subject was below his interest nor beyond his comprehension. For him, education was a journey, not a destination.

When he recovered, his left leg was about an inch shorter than his right, so he adapted to walking on the ball of his foot to maintain equilibrium. So well did he adjust to this mode of locomotion that few people were even aware of his defect.

As Dad's accident provided a golden opportunity to pursue his quest for knowledge, so my accident some thirty-seven years later set in train a series of events that led me from the Sacramento depot to a homestead in northern Nevada, a bit of human jetsam washed up on the alkali flats of Mosquito Lake. Little did I know that I had reached the Promised Land of Learning.

CHAPTER 3

"Here in this island we arrived; and here
Have I, thy schoolmaster, made thee more profit
Than other princes can. . . ."

The Tempest, Act I, Scene II
William Shakespeare

For the first few days after my arrival, we were confined to the house, except for Dad's brief excursions outside to tend the livestock and to empty night waste.

Then one night I was awakened by the sound of running water: off the roof, down the walls, under the house, everywhere a gurgle, a trickle, or a drip. Overnight, a Chinook wind had melted most of the snow. Like magic, fences, corrals, outbuildings, livestock, trees, rocky outcroppings, and mountain ranges materialized from their snowy confinement, and the valley floor became a lake.

While exploring this new wonderland, Dad told me that Old Roanie was due to calve soon and if she delivered a white heifer calf it was mine. Since she had always produced roan Durham bull calves in the past, the odds were not favorable. But Old Roanie was special. She was the sole survivor of the rabies epidemic which wiped out the rest of the dairy herd. Three rabid coyotes had gotten into the corral one night and bitten all of the cows but one before Old Leo, our shepherd dog, killed the Marauders. Although victorious, he did not escape unscathed. His heavy fur was ripped and torn. Fearing that he, too, would contract the dread disease, he was chained in the barn for weeks. Miraculously, he did not develop hydrophobia.

Despite the odds, Old Roanie gave birth to a beautiful white heifer calf, and I became a livestock owner. Naturally she was named Snowball.

About the same time that Snowball arrived, the first buttercups opened their golden chalices to the spring sun. Mother led the way between sage-brush and around boulders to the rocky knoll north of the house to pick a bouquet. Never having walked on rough terrain before, I had difficulty keeping up, which intensified her impatience at having to stop and wait for me. Eventually, we reached our El Dorado, collected our bounty, and headed home. As everyone knows, going downhill is even more difficult than going up, so it wasn't surprising that I slipped and fell, becoming wedged between two rocks. When I couldn't extricate myself, I called to Mother to help me. She stopped, looked back, and then continued on her way. I have no idea how long I struggled to free myself, but it was long enough to internalize a very valuable lesson: *never* ask for help, a learning experience that I never forgot.

Spring also brought Dad a government commission to capture baby antelope for the Save the Antelope program initiated by the Boone and Crockett Club[10] of New York City, and funded by E. S. Brownell, San Francisco game conservationist and capitalist, and William T. Hornaday, Curator of the New York Zoological Gardens, to pay the expenses for capture, rearing, and shipment of the antelope,[11] to be distributed among the national parks in the United States. Recipients of the restocking program included the Grand Canyon, Arizona; The Bison National Park in Moriese, Montana; and the Niobrara Game Refuge in Valentine, Nebraska.[12] The yearling "Lopey," last year's orphan, was shipped to the Wind Caves in South Dakota,[13] where tourists fed him cigarette stubs until he died of nicotine poisoning. Tobacco plays no favorites.

E. R. Sans, biological assistant in charge of the Nevada Biological Survey, was field inspector of the project.[14]

While waiting for the kidding season to start, Dad fenced five acres of brush and native grasses with six-foot woven wire, under the misapprehension that pronghorns were high jumpers like deer. While the *Antilocarpa americana* is the second fastest animal on four legs (the cheetah still holds the world record for speed), he/she goes through around, or under obstacles, not over.

When the kidding season began, north of Mosquito, Dad enlisted the help of his foster son, George Wood, and the Hapgood boys, True and Jesse. On horseback and leading pack animals equipped with alforjas, the men approached the "maternity ward" with caution and then waited motionless until the animals' natural curiosity overcame their fear. Then the men could move slowly about their business without stampeding the herd. Since the young can run within a few hours of birth, time is a crucial factor in their capture. Dad's policy was to select one of twins whenever possible. In this way, the mother still had a kid to rear, and the genetic pool of the relocated animals would be skewed to multiple births and faster population growth. Forty-one kids were transported to their new home in saddle bags. Thirty-nine survived. For three months, we bottle-fed our charges twice a day. The milking, feeding, and bottle-washing became an endless cycle. As the kids matured, a grain supplement was added to their diet.

As usual, ignorance played a role in the misdiagnosis of the problem, diminution of the antelope population, and its solution. To illustrate this sophism was the report by the gentleman who discovered the skeletons of two adult antelope in northern Washoe County[15] which were later sent to a biological museum in Amsterdam, Holland. Coincident with his discovery of the bones, the man observed an antelope chasing a coyote. From this, he deduced that the coyote had killed the defunct specimens. Only a bureaucrat could jump to such a conclusion, but it added weight to the popular misconception that coyotes were responsible for the decline of the antelope herds.

The truth of the matter was that the "encroachment of sheep" was determined to be the real threat to the antelope in Washoe County, not coyotes.[16] This belated wisdom eventually led the Boone and Crockett Club to start buying up land for a game preserve which later became the Charles Sheldon Antelope Refuge.

However, the care of antelope did not monopolize all of our attention. Like the rest of civilization, we were horrified by the kidnapping and "thrill" killing of fourteen-year-old Bobby Franks by Nathan Leopold, Jr., and Richard Loeb. Since Dad's hero, Clarence Darrow, was retained for the defense, we followed the case closely.

Loeb and Leopold were "rich, academically precocious and homosexual."[17] They started with "minor crimes: breaking windshields, [arson] , petty theft . . ."[18] culminating in the experimental murder of Loeb's cousin to test their own reactions to committing a capital crime. Darrow "could not risk a jury trial as . . . mental illness had never been allowed as a defense in American courts,"[19] so he pled the boys guilty, with mitigation, in a non-jury trial.[20] Four months later, Loeb and Leopold were sentenced to life imprisonment. Loeb was cut to death by a fellow inmate in 1936 and Leopold was paroled in 1958.

In addition to the coverage in the press, we bought *Little Blue Books*, published in Girard, Kansas, at five cents each, minimum order twenty for a dollar, postpaid. While these literary jewels featured mainly non-fiction and classics, transcripts of high-profile trials were also available.

At the local level, preparations were being made to celebrate Independence Day by having a rodeo at Home Ranch some six miles south of Vya. Originally the headquarters for the Miller and Lux cattle company in Nevada, Home Ranch was now owned by Martin Espil, sheepman. It had the necessary stables, chutes, and corrals to accommodate the traditional ropin,' ridin,' and bull-doggin' contests. The lack of bleachers posed no problem as the men perched on the top rails of the corrals while the women caught up on the latest gossip, arranged a smorgasbord of "vittles" on a trestle table, and kept a weather eye on their offspring.

The event attracted a large crowd, most of whom I did not know, being a newcomer. After all, Bald Mountain precinct now boasted eighty registered voters[21] and their families plus drifters and visitors.

Of course, no rodeo is complete without its "outlaw" horse or bull, the animal that had never been ridden, the one that would make a successful bronc-rider's reputation. The Home Ranch rodeo was no exception.

Also present was an illegal beverage, smuggled in by some of the cowboys to give them Dutch courage. Without its wit-addling influence, it is unlikely that the riders would have countenanced the suggestion to "stack the deck" in favor of the rider of the "outlaw" by tying his feet together under the horse's belly. Dad tried to dissuade them from their madness, but alcohol has no reason. It is also questionable if Miguel Bengochea, 26, newly arrived from Spain,[22] understood the new culture well enough to make a reasoned decision.

In any event, Miguel mounted up, the chute gates opened, and the "outlaw" horse burst forth in a flurry of side-winding, sun-fishing, and crow-hopping, designed to unseat his rider. When these maneuvers failed, he lay down and rolled on his hapless rider. Unable to escape because of his feet being tied, Miguel sustained fatal internal injuries before he was cut free and carried from the arena by four of his new friends. I followed them to the bunkhouse, but was not allowed inside. Nor was Mrs. Kemble who believed that abdominal massage was a panacea for any condition. Upon hearing her offer to massage the dying man, the response from inside was, "Keep that old bitch out of here!" I was shocked by such language and embarrassed for her son, Paul, who was inside with the dying man.

My eavesdropping was interrupted by Dad, who said that it was time to go home. He was terribly upset by the tragedy and his failure to prevent it.

A few days later "Uncle Jim" Flaugher, coroner, came up to our place to report on the inquest held at Vya, Nevada, July 7, 1924. Forrest Parry, his son-in-law, was listed as informant on the Certificate of Death.[23] Again I was excluded, so imagine my surprise when I read in the *Nevada State Journal* that Miguel Bengochea had committed suicide by gunshot.[24] One can't help wondering if this "suicide" was assisted suicide, mercy killing, or conspiracy to protect the living from the consequences of their negligence.

Whatever the truth about his demise, Miguel now rests in the Cedarville cemetery. J. F. Kerr, mortician, handled the arrangements.

On one of our trips to town, I met Maxine Hill, the daughter of Mother's friend, Lola Hill, and former resident of Long Valley. Maxine and I became life-long friends. To overcome the same name problem, I called her Packy and she called me Mac. She was six months younger than I and living proof that sweets do not cause fat or cavities. Her idea of a balanced diet was a candy bar in each hand. My sweet tooth was satisfied with ice cream once or twice a year, yet I was the one with weight and dental problems.

On our infrequent trips to Cedarville, I was always provided with "pin" money. My first "pin" money was a fifty-cent piece (equivalent to ten dollars today). I brought home half. Pleasantly surprised by my thrift, Dad gave me five dollars the next time we went to town. Again I only spent half. Even ants and bees have sense enough to prepare for a rainy day.

As it turned out, even shopping was not without risk. In the store, Mother and I were behind another mother and daughter at the checkout counter. I had been admiring the little girl and wishing that I had a sister like her when the clerk asked her her name. I did not catch the first name but the last was Gray. So when the clerk asked me my name, I was in a dilemma: admit that I didn't know my own name or tell a lie and give the Wood surname. I liked the name Gray and for all I *knew* it could be my name, so I said, "Maxine Gray." Mother's gasp told me that I had done it again! Out on the sidewalk, her mortification erupted. It seems that Mr. Gray was doing time in the penitentiary for some grievous crime. In the future, I was to use the Wood name even if it was a lie, until we learned my "real" name.

In August, E. R. Sans and E. S. Brownell[25] visited our ranch to check on the antelope project. While there, Mr. Brownell was impressed by my intelligence and artistic ability. Later he returned with his wife and told Dad that they wanted to adopt me. My orphan status was common knowledge, so the Brownells felt that the offer was not inappropriate. Dad said that it was my decision. He explained to me that the Brownells were wealthy and could provide greater educational opportunities than he and mother could. Also the Brownells were probably five to ten years younger.

The conference took place in the kitchen-dining area, so I went into the living room and hid behind the door to consider the offer. Compared to my former isolation, how could anyone be wealthier than I was already? There were all those books, newspapers, phonograph records, radio, my own room, and pets galore, both wild and domestic. What more could anyone want? Besides there was a certain obligation to the folks who had taken me in when no one else wanted me, so I opted for the status quo.

Although there had been talk of making a movie of the antelope project, nothing ever materialized, so in mid September Dad transported the antelope the 240 miles from Diessner to Reno by truck.[26] From Reno, Dad and Ernest Swanson, federal employees, accompanied the animals to their destinations by train.[27] Twelve antelope made the thousand mile trip to the Grand Canyon National Park, eighteen others went to the Bison National Park in Montana where they later died of foot-rot, and ten found a new home at the Niobrara Game Refuge in Valentine, Nebraska.[28]

When Dad returned, he brought Mother another china cup and saucer set for her collection and for me two horned toads from Arizona.

A large galvanized wash-tub served as a temporary vivarium for my new pets. I knew that horned toads were insectivorous, but I was unprepared for their inactivity. They depended on inertia and camouflage to attract their prey. Observing them was on a par with watching grass grow, but Mother's white cat, also named Snowball, was fascinated by these strange "critters." She would stand up with her forepaws on the rim of the tub and watch them for hours. Not being sure of her motivation, I watched her more than the toads. At least she would blink occasionally or twitch her tail. Then one day, I glimpsed her coming down the hill with something wriggling in her mouth. It was a live lizard. She carried it to the tub and dropped it in. Whatever her motivation, it was not predacious and she obviously knew her taxonomy.

Among my more lovable, and active pets were two groundhogs that Dad had rescued when he was tearing down an old building. They fit snugly into a kitchen match box and still had their eyes closed. We anticipated feeding problems but it was wasted worry. They stood up on their hind legs, grasped the bowl of the spoon in their front paws, and sucked up the warm milk greedily. The one with a white blaze on its nose was male and named Benny and the female was called Tiny G for Mrs. Kemble. Now that fall had come, the groundhogs were roly-poly fat, ready for their long winter hibernation, but not together. Benny reverted to the wild and made a new home in the rimrocks high above our house. Tiny G made her den under our house.

Coincident with the woodchucks' hibernation was the wheat harvest, a cooperative effort by the local ranchers. The mowers, rakers, and hay-wagons relied on live horse power, but the stationary rig which separated the grain from the chaff used gasoline. This new-fangled machine was set up near the Elmer Hill place and Dad was given the job of keeping it running. Several five-gallon cans of gasoline and a bucket of water for thirsty workers were placed in the shade created by the throbbing monster which spewed chaff in one direction and funneled kernels of wheat in another. After the truck was filled with its golden cargo and sent on its way to the flour mill in Surprise Valley, a canvas was spread on the ground under the grain spout to keep the growing pyramid of wheat from touching the earth until the truck returned.

It was a hot, still day. Nothing moved except the workers in the field, and rivulets of perspiration down our backs. Then suddenly a ripple of motion swept across the standing grain as if a gentle breeze had passed by, but there was no breeze where we were and no tremor beneath our feet to indicate a major earthquake. Dad, Mother, and I stared in wonder until we felt activity about our ankles and looked down. The ground was literally alive with thousands of chipmunks swarming around the pile of grain, filling their cheek pouches, and running off. Without immediate intervention, our winter's supply of flour and animal feed would be gone. Their vast numbers reminded Dad of the lemmings' devastating migration to the sea, and sea meant water. Quickly, he snatched the dipper from the water bucket and leaned it against the outside of the pail like a ramp. Instantly, the chipmunks started running up the ramp and tipping into the water. While Mother and I ran back to the water troughs near the corrals for more water, Dad gathered sticks and tools for make-shift ramps and cut the tops out of the empty fuel cans to make more water traps. As soon as the containers were filled with drowned chipmunks, they were dumped, and the cans refilled with water. This process continued until after dark when all the grain was threshed and our crop saved with a minimum of loss and no environmental fall-out as occurred in the "Nevada Mouse Plague of 1907-08." In that case, "the wheat was treated with yellow phosphorus in carbon bisulphid, a cheap and effective poison for field mice, but inflammable, explosive, and dangerous to birds. As a result . . . California quail were decimated, and magpies, crows, meadow larks and other seed-eating birds suffered . . . also many skunks and domestic cats were killed as a result of eating poisoned mice. Cases of fatal poisoning of livestock were frequent. The damage was estimated at $300,000."[29]

Whether these over-populations of rodents were the direct result of over-control of their natural predators, coyotes, may be unprovable, but the effects were consistent with man's short-term vision in dealing with natural resources. Like the three blind men, their interpretation of the universe is based on a minuscule part of the whole. Little wonder that their inductions are fallible.

In the good old days, childhood was the time spent preparing for responsible adulthood. Rights were not automatic. They were earned by demonstrating responsibility. I was kept busy taking care of my room, helping to feed the antelope, learning to milk a cow, carrying water from the well in a five-pound lard bucket, sawing juniper limbs with a bucksaw, setting the table, ironing napkins and handkerchiefs with flatirons heated on the kitchen range (the ironing board was placed between two chair seats to accommodate my short stature), washing clothes on a wash-board, *ad infinitum*. In fact, performing all adult tasks, modified to suit my size. There were no drones in our household. The devil would have been hard-pressed to find idle hands on the Double-X spread. On the other hand, there were rewards. I was allowed to read as late as I liked as long as I was up, dressed, combed, and brushed in the three-minute time limit after being called, the first step in learning punctuality. This is not cruel and unusual punishment. Children want to become adults. Only parents want them to stay forever young. The tobacco companies know that the most irresistible advertising to minors is "Adults only." Parents could use this psychology for better purposes. "Monkey see, Monkey do," is the earliest learning process. From day one, baby tries to imitate its parents, so being a good role model is the first rule in parenting. If Monkey watches sex and violence on television all the time, Monkey is bound to emulate some of it. However, we must give the devil his due. Television programmers are great environmentalists. Look at all the garbage they recycle.

CHAPTER 4

"But thou art fair; and at thy birth, dear boy,
Nature and fortune join'd to make thee great:
Of nature's gifts thou mayst with lilies boast,
And with the half-blown rose: . . ."

King John, Act III, Scene I
William Shakespeare

To understand the relationship, or lack thereof, between Mother and me, we must delve into the past. She and Dad were married in Smithville, South Dakota, in 1896. Later they migrated west to Washington and were living in Spokane by 1906, where Dad operated a shooting gallery. After ten years, they were still childless, so Mother started looking for an adoptee. Her search led her to a Catholic orphanage, where she found George, a puny, sickly two-year-old. He had been abandoned as a newborn infant on the proverbial church step, wrapped in quality swaddling clothes and the name Ross inscribed on one of his baby shoes. However, a local investigation of the name proved fruitless. Since baby clothes tend to be outgrown rather than worn out, they frequently are handed down, or to be politically correct, recycled. Therefore, the name Ross may have had no relationship to George. Other speculation linked him to "theater people." This theory gained credence later when he sang publicly on the stage in Spokane at the age of four.

After a lengthy interview with the Sisters and signing of necessary documents, Mother was allowed to take George home on a trial basis. Dad said that he was a basket case, scrawny with a runny nose, sores all over his body, asthmatic, and food-challenged. Nothing agreed with him. Hindsight indicates a typical milk allergy, but since allergies hadn't been invented yet, his condition went undiagnosed.

The first thing that Mother did was to put him on a diet of sugar and water or watered brandy. As the symptoms began to clear up, she expanded her trial-and-error experiment with other foods introduced one at a time for a brief period of time, very brief if it triggered a reaction. Eventually a safe menu was developed and he thrived.

With his immediate dietary problems resolved, Dad began to worry about the future. In a macho-dominated society, George's small size, blonde curls, big blue eyes, and golden voice might make him the target of bullies, or worse, so he initiated a regimen of breathing exercises and calisthenics to build him up physically. As he matured, he was trained in the manly art of self-defense so that he could defend himself if necessary. Because of his innate good nature, he made friends rather than enemies, and fisticuffs were unnecessary. The exception to the rule occurred when he was eighteen. Luther and Bill Pruitt, cowhands on a neighboring ranch, had a bad habit of leaving the gates open, resulting in livestock getting out and mixing with range herds. Labor-intensive effort was required to round up and separate the animals. After one such incident, Dad and George met Luther and Bill near one of our gates which they had neglected to close.

After the initial "Howdy," Dad said, "I'd appreciate it if you would close the gates behind you. It makes a lot of extra work when the stock get out."

Luther sneered. "Think you're big enough to make me?"

Dad said, "I can try." And the men dismounted.

Luther was twenty years younger and had a tough reputation as a brawler. He started toward Dad, when George stepped between them and said, "You look about my size."

Actually Luther was about thirty pounds heavier and in his prime. He figured he could make mincemeat of this stripling and finish off Dad as a dessert. He aimed a roundhouse swing at George, who wasn't there. While he was recovering his balance, George hit him several times, and wherever he hit him he left a small oval cut. The impact of the first blow had dislodged one of the flat stones in his ring, leaving a miniature cookie cutter. In the heat of battle, neither was aware of it until Luther was knocked down in defeat, all according to the Queensberry rules of self-defense. When George challenged Luther, Dad said to Bill, "Well, I guess that leaves you and me." But Bill was already having second thoughts about tangling with Dad, and he backed off.

When Luther was able to mount up, they left, after carefully closing the gate. Dad and George tried to find the missing gem in the dust stirred up by the fight but were unsuccessful.

Although George never fought in the ring, he later trained his 'cousins,' Herb and Neil Wood, who did compete in the local boxing matches.

Little wonder that Mother was besotted with her fair-haired boy. Except for food, her universe revolved around George.

Little wonder, too, that twenty years later she felt trapped by a careless remark into taking home an ugly duckling like me: big for my age, healthy as a horse (bad teeth, irregularity, and nearsightedness hardly qualified as major medical), straight dark brown hair, brown eyes, and worst of all, I couldn't carry a tune in a bushel basket!

Hence, I became a literal whipping-boy for her menopausal frustrations, a pastime she was careful to indulge only when Dad was away from home, because he did not believe in corporal punishment. She also threatened more dire consequences if I told. I didn't tell, but not because of fear. I knew that I was the cuckoo in the nest and had no family rights. Certainly I had no right to stir up more trouble between husband and wife. She already resented Dad's attention to my academic pursuits. She had no use for books, not even cook books, and distrusted anyone who did.

Dad took her verbal abuse stoically and I tried to endure her spankings with a stiff upper lip, but invariably tears gave me away, so then I got the bargain special—two for the price of one. The first paddling for the original infraction, real or imagined, and the second for crying. Her paddle of choice was an ivory-handled hair-brush, with a wooden butter-paddle running a close second.

One of my worst crimes was getting into her cosmetics. When she caught me red-handed, she went ballistic. I was a whore and a harlot and I was trying to take her husband away from her. Even given that I was the large economy size, I was still only four years old and ugly to boot. My response to her irrationality was to spend most of my time out-of-doors when Dad was gone, which luckily for him was most of the time.

When he was a Government trapper, he tended the traplines year round, taking only the coyote scalps and recording the stomach contents to justify the bureaucrats' premise to Congress that coyotes were dangerous predators. Unfortunately, the stomach contents did not substantiate this premise. The thousands of coyotes that strayed into Dad's traps ate only

insects, rodents, and occasionally a rabbit. He never found a single trace of
sheep, antelope, or other livestock. Dad described coyotes as Nature's K. P.s
(kitchen police) helping the vultures and magpies clean up the carrion that
occurs naturally in the wilds. When some of the officials suggested that he
enrich the coyotes' diet in his reports so that the program would not lose its
funding, Dad said that when he found evidence of farm or game animals,
he would report it. Needless to say, the funding for *his* contract renewal ran
out.

After that, he trapped only in winter when the pelts were prime. Part
of my education included the fleshing, stretching, and drying of the furs for
sale to itinerant buyers like Pugsley or direct to fur companies. He also
carried the mail from Vya to Diessner twice a week, Mondays and
Thursdays. Minnie Diessner was Postmaster from February 13, 1923, until
October 31, 1933, when the postal service was discontinued between Vya
and Diessner.[30]

Few homesteads were self-sustaining and moon-lighting
opportunities were limited. Besides trapping and mail carrying, Dad leased
grazing land to sheepmen and boarded the school teacher when there were
five and a half pupils to qualify for county funding. In 1924, there were
only two possibles, my foster cousins, Neil and Herbert Wood. Wallace and
Dorris were too old and Diessners' four girls, Amelia, Olga, Emma, and
Bertha, and I were too young so the school house stood empty that year.

Of my four 'cousins,' Wally was my favorite. He took time to play
"pretend" games with me, but I always felt sorry for Neil, the youngest of
the four siblings living with Uncle Ardie. The other seven children were
living with their mother, Clara, in Sandpoint, Idaho, where Dad had bought
them a house for $600.00. Neil was normally bright but cursed with
gullibility. He believed what he was told, so he was the perfect target for
sucker jokes and pranks by his older siblings and frequently was blamed,
and punished, for their misdeeds as well. Since Ardie did not believe in
sparing the rod, beatings were a way of life for Neil. To postpone, if not
escape, this abuse, he often visited Uncle Oat and Aunt Mattie, as my foster
parents were called by everyone, relative or not. He was five years older
than I so he could easily walk the distance between our adjoining ranches.
This trek had become a common practice long before I arrived on the scene.
In fact, one of these earlier visits nearly ended in disaster. As he neared our
house, a rabid bobcat burst out of the underbrush and pursued him.
Fortunately for him, the gun that hung above the kitchen door was not

unloaded and the ammunition safely locked away. George grabbed the rifle and shot the bobcat as it crossed the threshold just behind Neil. In an emergency an empty gun was useless and emergencies seldom give advance notice. All weapons were kept loaded and treated with respect. There were no "accidents" based on the excuse that they didn't know the gun was loaded. The rule, cast in concrete, was never to aim a gun or pull the trigger unless you meant to kill. No excuses, no exceptions. And no hand-guns.

When I joined the family, I fell heir to George's .22 rifle and 410 shotgun. There was no ammo wasted on target practice. I was issued one round and expected to bring home food for the table, usually a sagehen or young ground-hog. Rabbits had warbles and were off-limits. With only one shell, the prey had to be stalked and dispatched at close range. The game was skinned and gutted immediately, carried home, and placed in a pan of salt water. From there to the table was Mother's responsibility. Then I cleaned the gun and put it away in the closet. As survival training, hunting has its place, but I had no stomach for killing and soon gave up the practice altogether. Today, the only things that I can kill without remorse are houseflies, mosquitos, and dandelions.

But I, too, was guilty of unkindness. One day Neil offered to read the newspaper to me. After a few minutes of listening to his halting performance, I said, "Here, let someone read it who can," and proceeded to do so. Later, I was so ashamed of my insensitive behavior that I still regret it. Neil, on the other hand, was so conditioned to such treatment that he didn't seem to notice. He even beamed with pride at my achievement.

Although George and I were reared by the same foster parents, we had little in common. He was married, had a son, Donald, and was getting a divorce by the time we met, when he helped Dad capture the antelope. I rarely saw him but when I did, our relationship was based on mutual respect.

As nineteen twenty-four drew toward its close, I turned five and heard about Christmas for the first time. According to current tradition, a roly-poly character in a red suit and long white beard, drove a sleigh with eight reindeer through the sky on Christmas eve distributing gifts to all the children in the world. In my opinion, it was logistically impossible and I didn't believe a word of it. However, I decided to play along for their benefit. I played pretend games so if the folks wanted to observe the holiday in this manner, it was their right.

A ceiling-high juniper tree was installed in the corner of the living room and decorated with candles, tinsel, and ornaments, with a star on top.

To perpetuate the myth, Dad secretly rigged up sleigh bells outside which could be manipulated from inside when Santa passed over our house.

Always a light sleeper, I was awakened even earlier than usual on Christmas morning by Mother moving about in the living room. My bedroom door had been left ajar so that the heat from the stove could keep out the chill, and through the crack I could see her tucking the gifts about the tree, confirming what I already knew. I feigned sleep until she called me for breakfast and pretended surprise at Santa's gifts.

On January 6, 1925, the folks and I attended the wedding of George and his foster cousin, Dorris Wood, at the M. E. Parsonage in Cedarville, California.[31] After the ceremony, the pastor had the newlyweds jump over a broomstick held horizontally about twelve inches from the floor.

Unknown to me at the time was the fact that this was their second wedding ceremony. The first occurred September 8, 1923, eleven days before his divorce from Uintah Caldwell Wood was granted. Uintah filed the divorce action May 3, 1923, and married her first cousin, Jack Caldwell, six days later.[32]

Shortly after their second ceremony, George and Dorris homesteaded the 640 acres adjacent to our south boundary and built their new home, the first in Mosquito Valley with indoor plumbing.

In due course, Dorris became pregnant and often spent time with Mother and me when Dad and George were away from home working. One such visit coincided with Dad's birthday, June 10. Although she was only three months *en ciente*, she was already taking advantage of her "condition" to avoid helping Mother with the dishes that evening. Instead, she was playing solitaire on the small table placed near the open living room door. I was standing on the opposite side of the table, watching. After several games, darkness had fallen and Mother lit the coal oil lamp to provide illumination. Dorris gathered up the deck again and started to shuffle the cards. As she did so, one card floated out of the deck and slowly wobbled its way through the doorway into the living room.

"Damn!" said Dorris, slamming down the rest of the deck and getting up to retrieve the fallen card. Fumbling around in the dark without success, she called to Mother to bring the lamp. The light was brought, but the card could not be found. Mother asked what had happened. When Dorris explained and I verified her account, Mother declared that it was a present'ment [sic].

"Oh, Aunt Mattie," groaned Dorris who did not believe in paranormal phenomena, "you and your present'ments!"

Mother just said, "Count your cards." Dorris argued but finally did so. Then she counted them again. And again. There were fifty-two. Mother went to the calendar and wrote the time on the date. Dorris went on playing and the incident was forgotten until a couple days later when we spied a dust cloud on the road to the south. It was a Messenger on a motorcycle bringing a telegram for Dorris. Her newly married sister, Ivy Wood Turner, had died two days before in Ontario, Oregon. Dorris maintained that Mother's "present'ment" was just a coincidence. Her denial might have carried more weight if it had been an isolated case, but Mother had a history of psychic revelations. One such incident occurred not long after she and Dad were married. They lived several miles from town and traveled by horse and wagon. On one of their trips to town they visited with some of their friends in Sturgis, who had a child called Gypsy. It was late by the time they got home and they were soon asleep in bed. In the middle of the night, Dad was awakened by Mother poking him in the ribs.

"Otho, wake up. Wake up! Gypsy is dead!" Groggy with sleep, he tried to persuade her that she had had a bad dream and to go back to sleep, but Mother was adamant, so he got up, dressed, harnessed up the horses, and drove back to their friends' house. When they arrived, the house was all lit up and the family in a state of grief and shock. Gypsy was indeed dead.

Prior to the June 10th "coincidence," Dad had leased our grazing land to sheepman, "Fat" Martin Lartirigoyan. After lambing, the sheep were moved to our ranch by a young Basque herder named Joe. When I saw "Fat" Martin coming to replenish Joe's camp supplies, I would run out to open the barbed wire gate for him and his pack burro. In exchange for this service, I was added to the burro's burden and transported back to the house. While he and Dad were visiting, he would bounce me on his knee and say, "Probobably [sic] you're a very fine girl."

Soon I was tagging after Joe and the sheep. He was eager to learn English and I to learn Spanish, a win-win situation, but Mother soon put a stop to it. Joe was a "furriner" and therefore suspect. When I went to tell him that I couldn't tutor him anymore, he said, "I see." Then, "Wait." He quickly sorted out a half dozen ewe lambs and a buck for me.

"Keep them, and by the time you grow up, you will be a rich woman."
I was willing to follow this road to riches, but circumstances did not permit.
However, I was in the sheep business for a couple of years. As they say,

> *"A whistling girl and a band of sheep*
> *Are the best company a man can keep."*

CHAPTER 5

"The evil that men do lives after them;
The good is oft interred with their bones."

Julius Caesar, Act III, Scene II
William Shakespeare

After the tragedy of the previous Fourth of July at Home Ranch, plans were made for a less ambitious observance of our Independence, to be held at our place. Dad constructed a brush arbor in the front meadow by setting up corner posts and roofing it with green aspen boughs. Under it were picnic tables and benches. The phonograph was moved outdoors to fill in between live music and vocalists. While horseshoe pitching, arm wrestling, and kindred activities occupied the mature males, the young men clambered up the mountain behind our house where the snow never melted to get ice and snow to freeze the home-made ice cream. My function was to keep turning one of the freezer handles as others added ice and rock salt to the thawing slush between the central container and the outer wall of the freezer. Neil manned another. Can't remember who did the honors on the third gallon. The reward for this tedious, and seemingly endless, task was to lick the dasher after it was removed from the frozen ice cream.

After everyone had over-eaten to the point of discomfort, Mother brought out her Eastman Kodak to immortalize the occasion in black and white. One of these snapshots shows me dancing in a white frock made in the latest style, drop-waisted with box-pleated skirt. No one would ever suspect that that frock was once a survey map inked on fine linen which Dad had found at an abandoned homestead and carried home to preserve for posterity. Mother had no interest in posterity. She soaked the ink from the cloth and converted it into a dress for me.

Even having my picture taken (which I hated) could not spoil my love of dancing, my first and most enduring pleasure in life. Although ballet was my first choice of career, my mirror confirmed that I wasn't built for it, so I settled for my second love, reading, which had no physical limitations. Even the blind can read in Braille.

Among our many guests at the celebration were the Kembles who lived about ten miles south of us in Long Valley. Their family included Albert and Tiny G., sons Carl and Paul, daughter Eunice, and grandson, Carey, also orphaned. Carey was a year younger than I and about half my size. Our friendship had gotten off to a bad start the previous year when he was three and I was four. Due to circumstances beyond our control, we were forced to spend the night at the Kembles' home. While there was no lack of hospitality, beds were in short supply, so Carey and I had to share a cot, he at one end and I at the other, our feet barely touching. This arrangement violated his sense of the fitness of things and he declared that he wasn't going to sleep with no damned girl! And he didn't. He kicked me all night long, so neither of us slept. By day, he was my closest friend, but *nobody* was close enough to share his bed. Thankfully, no more emergencies arose to test his territorial imperative, and our friendship grew. When I visited his place, we played at cattle ranching, his large collection of marbles being the "cattle" and horseshoes representing "horses." Carey dreamed of a cattle ranch in Texas when he grew up and wanted me as a partner, but he made it abundantly clear that while we would probably have to get married "so people wouldn't talk," we didn't have to *live* together. If we tired of make-believe, we climbed over the fence into the bull pasture. Usually we waited until the white Durham bull was lying down, chewing his cud, before climbing on his back for a ride when he got up. Of course, we were forbidden to go near him. He had gored a man to death and was about to be destroyed, when Mr. Kemble offered to buy him and A. P. Norton agreed. The animal was dehorned and isolated in a six-foot-high wire enclosure except at breeding time. Carey and I were never caught riding the bull, but we were caught trying to rope the dairy calves. Catching them was easy but turning 'em loose was another matter, and we wound up with rope burns on our legs. Tiny G's treatment for rope burns was to prepare a bucket of hot water laced with Sloan's Horse Liniment and to thrust our legs into the steaming bath. Believe me, heroes are made, not born. We sat there shivering with shock and tears running down our faces, but we survived. I'm still not sure if the "cure" was punishment or therapy, but as behavior modification, if intended, it was a bust. We continued trying to emulate our elders and being punished for it.

While I knew very little about my "real" family, Carey's background was common knowledge. His father, Frank E. Page, had left a wake of motherless children behind him. Although Frank married Virginia Louise Dickson in 1905, there is no birth record for his son, Francis R. Page, born March 18, 1911,[33] who was "raised by his Aunt Virginia Dickson." On November 14, 1914, twins, Edith and Ethel Page, were born in Eagleville, California. Present at the delivery were Aunt Ethel McMahon and cousin, Thelma Archer.[34] Virginia Dickson Page died January 13, 1919, in labor, with pneumonia, attended by J. T. Meredith, M.D.[35] The five-year-old twins went to their Aunt Vine. Frank's next wife was Josephine Kemble who died December 14, 1920, of puerpual infection two months after the birth of their son, Carey. W. D. Coates was attending physician.[36] Given the circumstances, it was not surprising that Carey's maternal grandmother blamed Frank for Josephine's death. This belief was verbalized every time Carey misbehaved. Tiny G would douse him up and down in the cold spring water of the well, clothes and all, and say, "You're just like your murdering old father!"

In 1925, Frank Page and Pearl Connell were business partners in the management of Hotel Surprise on Main Street in Cedarville, California. That year, Page was arrested and fined, Case No. 2675, for sale of intoxicating liquor to an Indian.[37] Since Prohibition was still in effect, he also violated the Volstead Act in the transaction.

At the national level, education was on trial. A science teacher in Dayton, Tennessee, dared to teach the theory of evolution in the Bible Belt. Clarence Darrow defended Scopes against William Jennings Bryan. Scopes was convicted and fined one hundred dollars, but the decision was later set aside.

In Long Valley, Nevada, Leo Weilmunster was enforcing the game laws[38] when he wasn't setting a record in Washoe County as a Government trapper. His success as a trapper was attributed to his mode of transportation. Instead of a horse, he used a motorcycle which enabled him to extend his trap lines in summer.

Back at the ranch, summer drew to a close and fall brought an array of esteemed guests: James G. Scrugham, Governor of Nevada, 1923-27, and Publisher of the *Nevada State Journal*; Dr. P——— and his nurse from Pasadena, California; millionaire Charlie Karnes and wife, also a nurse;

and the current middle or welter weight boxing champion whose name eludes me. The Governor's schedule did not permit a prolonged visit, but he managed a short hunting trip followed by dinner with us. The table could be extended to accommodate a crowd but chairs couldn't, so the Governor perched on my armless high chair. When Mrs. Karnes insisted on plying him with personal service at the table, he finally exploded. "For God's sake, woman, sit down and let a man eat in peace!" She did, and he did.

Since paying for hospitality was taboo, departing guests usually "tipped" a youngster. The Governor gave me a dollar and the boxer donated a five when they left.

Dr. P——— and the Karnes' pitched their tents and stayed another week or two. When they departed, Dr. P——— contributed another five and the millionaire's wife scraped up 35 cents for me. I divided my "take" with Mother. She bought oilcloth to cover the walls and ceiling of the kitchen-dining room area, and I ordered a dress from Sears catalog.

Before he left, the doctor also gave Mother a free physical checkup and diagnosed Bright's disease, now called glomerulonephritis and hypertensive contracted kidney, and prescribed a strict diet, which she ignored.

Another distinguished visitor that year was Uncle Bob, Dad's youngest brother from Sturgis, South Dakota. Robert I. Wood, D.D.S., received his degree from the Chicago College of Dental Surgery in 1912 and taught dental anatomy there for two years before establishing his own practice in Sturgis in 1914. He enlisted in the United States Army Dental Corps in 1917 and served with the American Expeditionary Forces as Dental Surgeon with the 42nd Rainbow Division through his entire service. When he returned from France in 1919, he brought with him some German art books as his own hobbies were drawing and etching. When he saw my artistic efforts, he promised to send those books to me, which he did. Although they were printed in German, the same decoding process that I used in learning to read English soon broke the language barrier.

Later, Uncle Bob developed the dental prosthetic technique of using physiologic relief in maxillary impressions which brought him international recognition.

On a sadder note was the death of three-year-old Mildred A. Marriette of appendicitis. Dr. Kennedy had tried to persuade the parents to let him operate, but they trusted in God's will. Mother and I attended the funeral held at the Kerr Mortuary in Cedarville. I'll never forget the small casket draped with dark purple flowers and the overpowering fragrance.

School started in September with the four Diessner girls and me. The "half-student" was provided by short-time visitors such as Maxwell Marriette, when his mother substituted for a few weeks, or temporary school age boarders like Lucille and Tommy Royce.

The school day began with the Pledge of Allegiance, without the phrase "under God," which was not included until the Eisenhower administration in 1956. Then we sang *America*, followed by about five minutes of calisthenics to get our blood circulating before we settled down to work. I never attended a public school where prayer was allowed, let alone taught. Nor have I ever interviewed anyone who had prayer in a public school. In parochial or private schools, yes. Education was successful in the old days because of discipline, not prayer, not phonics, not the three R's. Discipline, and I do not mean corporal punishment, has been replaced by "excuse abuse" and misguided social policies. The military and private schools are still able to fulfill their functions because they still maintain discipline. Without it, the individual, the family, the school, and society as a whole are rudderless. In the old days, the standard of behavior was based on the choice between right and wrong, not "does it feel good."

While I remember all of my teachers: Kathleen O'Connell, Laura Lee Emerson (later Magnussen), Elsie Conners, Mrs. Killingsworth, and EllenGrace Dunn who later married Paul Kemble, some memories are more vivid than others. One day Miss Emerson, Lucille, Tommy, and I were walking home from school when Laura Lee suddenly stiffened out and fell to the ground like a plank. She sent us home to get help. While she was awaiting rescue, she was surrounded by curious antelope. Being a city girl, she was a bit apprehensive but survived their attention without lasting trauma. By the time George arrived in his car, she had struggled to a sitting position and could be helped into the vehicle. She was rushed to a hospital where she underwent emergency surgery for a ruptured appendix. She made a full recovery and returned to finish her teaching assignment.

In late October, Dorris, Mother, and I moved to Cedarville temporarily to await the arrival of the stork which was scheduled to deliver on my birthday, November 1, but like most delivery services was five days late. While we were waiting, I enrolled in the first grade, just in time to participate in some activity requiring crepe paper costumes. I think I was a tree, although the leaves were red, Autumnal photosynthesis? So maybe not. Granting that the exercise was intrinsically silly, as these performances usually are, we had not yet completely lost our marbles. No one yelled, "Rape! Murder!" when a little boy in the back row, Donald Quirk, kissed me on the nape of the neck. We were born a hundred years too soon, thank Heavens!

In like manner, Halloween was a night of amnesty for misbehavior as a reward for good behavior the other three hundred sixty-four days of the year. Young people could tip over outdoor privies, disassemble wagons and reassemble them on top of buildings, abscond with school bells, soap the windows, run around in sheets making weird noises, and feel deliciously wicked, but the occasion had not been elevated to extortion with threats of "Trick or treat." I realize that change is the only constant, but why can't anything ever change for the better?

My birthday "present" finally arrived, a six-pound niece named Violet Kathleen but always called "Georgie" because Mother thought that she looked like George, which she didn't.

Mother was experienced as a mid-wife but usually assisted Dr. Kennedy, who was a legend as a "baby doctor." Exceptions to the rule occurred when delivery was preceded by only one or two labor pains, which explains why Erno Benner made his debut January 14, 1926,[39] with mother officiating. Knowing that his mother, Hazel Benner, didn't believe in wasting time in labor, Mother and I had moved to the Benner home in Cedarville from the ranch to be available for the accouchement. When Dr. Kennedy arrived, he found everything in order, made a few notes on time of delivery and birth weight, and left. In a few days, Mother and I returned home.

The long winter evenings were not all spent reading. Sometimes, I listened to a children's program on KGO radio. When listeners were invited to write in, I did so. My letter was duly read and eulogized on the air.

Less successful was my order to Sears for a surrogate brother named Bobby Arthur. I knew that I had an older brother, Gene, and a younger half-brother, Tommy, somewhere, so I was always looking for them, especially Gene. My looking led me to the boys' suits being modeled by small boys in the catalog. I chose the one who most closely resembled Gene, filled out the order form, and mailed it. And waited. And waited.

Months later, Arthur Van Riper came to visit and Dad explained that he was my Bobby Arthur. He had been in stock so long that he had grown up, so he became my "big brother," a role that Arthur willingly maintained as long as I knew him.

That spring, Dad bought five or six hundred head of sheep instead of leasing out the grazing, so the "bummers" that Joe had given me the previous year now had company.

The Fourth of July came and went without incident, but on the seventh, we heard that Pearl Connell was missing. Call it a rush to judgment, but there was no doubt in Dad's mind that Frank Page was responsible. Pearl's body was found on Thursday, July 8, in an old cellar near the Bailey place . . . "choked and hit on the head with a blunt instrument."[40] "Earl Boston, constable, secured the crime scene, and the autopsy was performed by Doctors Kennedy, Coppedge, and Stiles."[41] The autopsy report read in part "that the deceased, 44-year-old Pearl Connell, weighed 150 pounds, measured 5'4" and died by strangulation, neck broken postmortem" with contusions and abrasions caused by a bloody rock found at the scene.[42]

Arrested were Frank E. Page, C. L. Unger, William Goodwin, and his sister, May Rose, and later released for insufficient evidence. Frank Page fled to the Bay area where he was arrested and returned to Modoc County.[43] Due to lynch threats, a heavy guard was placed over Page, Cedarville hotelman, suspected of the brutal murder of Pearl Connell, business associate.[44]

While we waited for due process to run its course, other events claimed our attention. In August, "W. A. Johnstone and F. E. Bush . . . purchased seven of the big stock ranches from Miller and Lux, all in Nevada."[45] Although I never knew the legendary Henry Miller himself (he died before I was born), we still enjoyed his largess. We ate Miller and Lux beef with his blessing and that of Charles Demick, his area manager in Nevada, and later brand inspector.

Heinrich Alfred Kreiser (Henry Miller) was born July 21, 1827, in Brackenheim, Germany.[46] At eight, he had a vision of the Double-H brand and endless herds of cattle.[47] At nineteen, he arrived in New York with $5.00 and went to work in a butcher shop where he worked sixteen-hour days and then studied English from 9-12 P.M. His pay was $8.00 per month.[48] There he met Henry Miller, shoe salesman, who was also trying to save ship fare to San Francisco. Miller got his ticket first and then changed his mind about going. He offered the ticket to his friend Kreiser for a reduced price who jumped at the offer. However, the ticket was made out to Miller and stamped "Non-transferable," so Kreiser became Miller. Later he legalized the name change. At thirty-one, he formed a partnership with Charles Lux, another butcher.[49]

Soon Miller and Lux "owned over one million acres of land in five states, over one million head of livestock, two banks and their branches, reservoirs, and other properties . . . appraised at fifty million dollars, acquired and developed by the sole efforts of one man."[50] He even had his own scrip!

Miller was one of the first to introduce Alfalfa, rice, and cotton to California,[51] and the Durham, Hereford, and Devon blend of cattle that he developed soon became synonymous with his name and brand.[52] He never drank, smoked, or carried a gun although he spent most of his time in the saddle in the West at its wildest. His partner, Charles Lux, supervised their meat processing plant in the Bay area and managed the social affairs for the firm.[53]

One of the primary trails for his spring and fall cattle drives between Oregon and Nevada passed our homestead and his riders enjoyed our hospitality on such occasions. Hence the *carte blanche* in the meat department.

In January 1911, Charles Demick was chosen as leader of the posse of twenty-two men mobilized to catch the killers of Harry Cambron, rancher, and three Basque sheep herders, John Laxague, Peter Erramouspe, and Bertrand Indiano, at Little High Rock canyon. Although rustlers were first suspected, evidence at the scene indicated an Indian ambush. After following a cold trail to Paradise Valley, four men left the posse because their horses gave out and Demick because of pressing Miller and Lux company business. The band of Shoshone Indians were finally located at Kelly Creek, Nevada. A shoot-out ensued, in which several Indians died. A survivor told her captors that the band had raided a Miller and Lux ranch, killed a Chinese cook, and stolen some horses before their ambush at Little High Rock Canyon.[54]

One of the posse members was Fred Hill, father of my friend, Packy. Like her, many of my high school classmates were relatives of the victims or of the posse. In fact, John Laxague, Jr., son of one of the victims, prominent businessman and former supervisor, still resides in Surprise Valley.

Other visitors who used the trail by our ranch were the Paiutes who summered at Massacre Lake some sixteen miles east of Vya and wintered at the Fort Bidwell reservation. One of these visits stuck in my mind because it contributed to my store of sign-reading and interpretation, another survival skill of the old West. An early snow storm had overtaken the first three riders that we saw, apparently two adults and a boy, but they did not stop. Later two more Paiute men stopped by for coffee and cookies. When Dad referred to the earlier travelers as two men and a boy, one of our guests corrected him.

"No, two men and an old man."

"Oh," said Dad, "you know them."

"No, we read sign in the snow."

"How?" asked Dad.

"Well, they make stop to relieve themselves. Boy spray all over. Old man pee straight down."

Even without a better mouse trap, the world seemed to beat a path to our door: a group from New England who had never seen an antelope before, two radio opera singers on their way from New York to San Francisco, Government officials, cowboys and Indians riding stirrup to stirrup in happy harmony, fur buyers, and traveling salesmen for Raleigh and Watkins products. But the most unexpected guest that year was my grandmother who "gave me away" two years earlier. The purpose of her visit was never clarified, but she did bring a few family pictures and a small vanity case for me. The photographs included wedding portraits of her and my grandfather, one of her and my brother, Gene, one of Gene and me together, and a snapshot of my mother. She told us that my half-brother, Tommy, had been adopted at birth by a doctor, unidentified, and that my mother had married a barber in the Bay area. My real father, Charles H. Tendering, was a Marine at Mare Island Naval Shipyard in Vallejo, California, during World War I. He was of German extraction and served as interpreter at the base. She gave us her address on Greenly Drive in Oakland but refused to disclose the current whereabouts of my mother and brother. After her visit, I wrote several letters to her, but she never responded. At least, I now knew my "real" name and it became the focus of my continuing quest for ancestral roots.

Of course, not all of our visitors came in friendship. One notable exception was Mr. H——, cattleman, who was moving his herd south early because of the drought. While his riders held the milling cattle in check, the owner came to the door to try to rent the forty acres south of Swancott's place that Dad owned. It had a big water hole and bunch grass knee high. He offered Dad twenty-five dollars for its use, but Dad told him that he was saving it for his own stock and did not want to rent it. Mr. H—— rode off in a huff. About a half hour after the herd moved on, Carey, who had been visiting us, decided that it was time to go home. As was customary, I would ride part way with him on Dad's favorite mount, old Leroy. We kept behind the dust cloud stirred up by the cattle. When we passed the Swancott place, we realized that the dust cloud had stopped, and the bellowing of milling animals reached our ears. Curious about this development, we slid off our horses and ground tied them in the tall sagebrush beside the road. Then, concealed by the dust, we crept forward to investigate. There we saw one of the riders cutting the wire to allow the stock access to our property. We hid in the tall brush until the cattle had sated their thirst, trampled the feed they did not eat, and continued on their way. Then we discussed what we should do. Cutting fences was a serious violation of the Western code and often precipitated range wars. We agreed not to report the incident, in the interest of peace, but to tell the truth if we were asked. We were never asked. Even then I was a pacifist.

CHAPTER 6

". . . but I tell you, my lord fool,
out of this nettle, danger,
we pluck this flower, safety."

> *King Henry* IV, Part I, Act II, Scene III
> William Shakespeare

On the credit side of the ledger fifteen years after the "massacre" at Little High Rock, my life was saved by the timely intervention of an elderly Paiute at Summit Lake Indian Reservation. In his role as Government trapper, Dad had to make periodic inspections of the area. As it was summer and the weather nice, Mother and I opted to accompany him. Unfortunately, the roads were better adapted to horses than cars, and Dad miscalculated the car's clearance and "high-centered" on a rock. The damage to the oil-pan was considerable. Since oil-pan gaskets don't grow on trees, or sagebrush either, we were stranded until we could order a replacement by a passing rancher en route to Reno. We made camp in the shade of the willows lining a feeder creek to the lake and I spent most of my time watching the "wild canaries" (American goldfinches) while we waited. Then I developed dysentery. While the folks were aware that I made frequent trips to the outdoor "facilities" (tall bushes or scrub juniper), they were not alarmed. Stomach upsets were common to small children. Luckily, an elderly Paiute read the sign differently. He told Dad that the "Indian babies were dying like flies" because of the bad water. The Indians were already leaving.

There was no time to wait for the rancher to return from Reno, so Dad blocked up the car, hammered the oil-pan back into shape with a rock, and cut up a new inner tube for a gasket. With this makeshift repair we managed to make it to Hanging Rock and good water. Without the kindly concern of a native American, I, too, would have "died like a fly."

Although the rabies epidemic had been subsiding, it was still taking a sporadic toll on livestock and humans. Oscar and Bertha Steward were managing Leonards Baths, eight miles north of Cedarville. Their two small children, seven-year-old Robert and five-year-old Charlotte (my second cousins), were playing around the pool when a rabid bobcat sprang on Robert's back. Maggie Jones, a patron, grasped the bobcat by the ears and pulled it off the boy and held it until it could be dispatched. Naturally, Robert had to take the two-week Pasteur treatment of shots. While thirty-four cases of people taking the treatment were reported in Lassen County, California, alone[55] only Robert took the shots twice, after being exposed a second time by a rabid puppy.

Closer to home, Dad also took the shots, which he blamed on negligence. He was repairing a fence line when he saw a coyote trotting along beside it. Almost automatically he shot and skinned it. Then he realized that the animal was rabid. Since Dad always worked without gloves, the barbed wire cuts on his hands were clearly visible, a fertile field for an invading virus. He went to Cedarville to get a kit of fourteen syringes of the anti-serum. Dr. Kennedy demonstrated the proper procedure for subcutaneous inoculation and sent Dad home with the other thirteen doses, to be self-administered.

On another occasion, Dad developed symptoms of jaundice and went to Dr. Kennedy for diagnosis. When he had finished his examination, Kennedy said, "Well, it could be one of three things, all of them fatal. I recommend that you consult another doctor." Dad said that Kennedy's word was good enough for him, but if he was going to die anyway, would the doctor care to experiment? His "kill-or-cure" prescription was to drink a quart of mineral oil a day for thirty days. Dad lived for another twenty years.

Dad was also his own dentist. When a molar started bothering him, he dug out the pliers and extracted it, without any pain-killer.

While the days were filled with coping with the present, the long winter evenings were frequently spent in reminiscence. The most memorable of Mother's experiences occurred shortly after she and Dad were married. Since Dad's job was some thirty miles away from their prairie home in Dakota Territory and too far to commute by horseback on a daily basis, a neighbor girl stayed with Mother when Dad was away. One evening, the girls entertained themselves by tying a water snake to a cat's tail. The poor cat went mad with fear, climbing the walls and yowling piteously, which the girls apparently found hilarious. Eventually, the cat shook off the snake and escaped through a window. Still chuckling at the cat's antics, the girls went to bed. During the night, Mother's left foot slipped off the side of the bed and a ten-foot diamond-back rattler struck it, sinking its fangs into her ankle. Like the cat, they panicked. Instead of applying a tourniquet and remaining quiet while her friend went for help, both girls ran the mile or so to a neighbor's farm, still clad in their nightgowns and barefoot. Mother was placed on a table, the fang marks lanced, and freshly killed chicken breasts applied to the wound. As soon as the meat turned black, another chicken poultice took its place. While these emergency measures were in progress, another member of the family rode to the ranch where Dad worked. Then Dad rode another sixty miles to the nearest doctor. By the time the doctor finally reached his patient there was little that he could do but have her transported to town where she was literally kept on ice for nearly a year before she recovered. Except for a fear of snakes, her ordeal had no lasting effect.

The high point in Dad's childhood memories was an unauthorized ride that he took in a parade. Living next door to Fort Meade after Custer's last stand at the Little Big Horn, Dad was familiar with Comanche, Captain Miles Keogh's horse, the sole survivor of that historic battle:

Of all that stood at noon-day
In the fiery, scorpion ring,
Miles Keogh's horse at evening
Was the only living thing.

And Sturgis issued the order,
Which future time shall read
While the love and honor of comrades
Is the soul of the soldier's creed.

He said: Let the horse, Comanche,
Henceforth till he shall die,
Be kindly cherished and cared for
By the Seventh Cavalry.

And at Regimental formation
Of the Seventh Cavalry,
Comanche draped in Mourning and led
By a trooper of Company "I"
Shall parade with the Regiment. "[56]

51

Naturally such an illustrious animal took pride of place in any military parade and accoutered in the military manner ordered by General Sturgis. On one such occasion, Dad was part of the crowd lining the parade route and standing beside a soldier. Imagine his surprise and delight when the soldier suddenly lifted him up and placed him in the empty saddle on Comanche's back and let him finish the ride back to the Army paddocks.

As a young man Dad signed on to one of those famous cattle drives, but the most exciting thing that occurred on his tour happened one night while he and another cowboy were riding night herd, circling the cattle in opposite directions, and singing to cover any sudden noises that might stampede the sleeping herd. All was quiet when he and his partner suddenly saw a ghost-like figure threading its way through the mesquite and cacti, straight toward the herd. Realizing the imminent danger of stampede if the cattle sighted the apparition, the men spurred forward to intercept this threat to the night's tranquility. On closer inspection, the "ghost" proved to be one of their own drovers walking in his sleep! Clad in white long-johns and bare-footed, he had negotiated the mile or so from camp without stepping on a single thorn, but that was the end of his good luck. He was fired on the spot, as a "clear and present danger" to the safe conduct of a cattle drive.

Of course, not all problems were settled so peacefully. Dad's sister, Annie, was the only girl in a household with five brothers, and the apple of her father's eye. When she was fifteen, she attracted the attentions of an unsuitable young man named George Goodspeed, a self-professed thief (he had misappropriated the proceeds of a sale of livestock entrusted to his care) and a frequenter of barrooms and brothels, exactly the type to appeal to a headstrong young girl. Her father pointed out that Annie was too young to be courted, but if Goodspeed's intentions were honorable he could wait until she was eighteen. While love can wait, lust cannot. Goodspeed continued to press his suit surreptitiously and Annie's father warned him that if he came near her again, he would be shot on sight. Goodspeed chose to ignore this warning. One fine morning in July, Annie and her mother were walking home from church, two miles away, when Goodspeed overtook them on horseback. He dismounted and walked the rest of the way with them. Annie's father saw them coming and was waiting at the gate.

"I told you to stay away from her," he said, and both men drew their weapons and fired simultaneously. Goodspeed was hit twice in the heart and once in the back as he fell. Wood was shot in the head and abdomen. Goodspeed died instantaneously, but Wood lived a couple hours. Before dying he asked if he had killed the s.o.b. Assured that he had, he died in peace.[57]

One can understand a person risking his life for his principles, but who can understand the fatal attraction of a bad man to a good woman? Dad maintained that the lack of understanding between the sexes was an innate safeguard for the perpetuation of the species. He said that if men and women really understood each other, the species would die out overnight. Maybe that explains the extinction of the dinosaurs; they lost their rosy-colored blinkers.

While lack of understanding characterizes the relationship between the sexes, misunderstanding is common to all. When a new man was hired on the ranch where Dad worked, practically the first question he was asked was, "What chances did a man have with the rancher's three daughters?" Dad's response was not encouraging. "There's no tellin' with women. They're just as apt to fall for a monkey as a man." The new man immediately misinterpreted this comment as casting aspersions on his ancestry, and Dad had considerable difficulty persuading the man that his comment was directed at the unpredictability of feminine preference, not the man's antecedents.

However, Dad's most embarrassing linguistic *gaffe* occurred while he was employed as an enumerator for the 1900 census, which coincided with an outbreak of smallpox. Dad was assigned to the rural population of the district and advised to reassure the householders that he had been vaccinated for the dread disease before he entered the residence. At his first stop, he identified himself through the closed door and started to add the prescribed assurance, but the word immunized eluded him and he blurted out that he had been circumcised! Instantly, he corrected himself but he never forgot the incident, not because of the sexual connotations as most people infer, but because he had made such a gross error. Being self-educated, he tended to be hypersensitive about his verbal skills.

Shortly after the turn of the century, he and Mother headed west, first to Coeur d'Alene, Idaho, then up to British Columbia, down to Bellingham, Washington, and back to Spokane where Dad operated a shooting gallery, and George joined the menage.

Dad told about the spawning run of sturgeon up the Columbia River "so thick that a man could walk across the river on their backs."

About 1909, Dad was stricken with rheumatoid arthritis and became bedridden. The doctor recommended a change of climate, so the folks loaded their belongings on a wagon and headed south. By the time they reached Nevada, Dad's rheumatism was gone, and never returned. Based on the Land Patent records in Reno, Nevada, Dad and Mother were the first settlers in Mosquito Valley, Township 45, N of Range 19, E of Mt. Diablo Meridian, Nevada. According to the Official Plat of the Survey, the homestead encompassed 278 43/100 acres. Perhaps this isolation explains why they missed the 1910 census of the Bald Mountain precinct of Washoe County. A year later, Elmer Hill staked out a claim of 315 46/100 acres at the south end of the valley. About 1920, Oscar George Diessner and family homesteaded 319 4/100 acres on the east side of the valley across from our place. In 1923, Dad's brother, Arden Wood, filed a claim of 462 26/100 acres adjacent to our north boundary line. When Arden surveyed his claim, he decided that Dad's survey was wrong and his fence was twenty feet too far north and therefore on Arden's land. Dad disagreed with the new survey but pointed out that the twenty-foot strip of sagebrush and alkali was hardly worth fighting over. But Arden was a man of conviction. He built a parallel fence twenty feet south of the existing one, which left the disputed land inaccessible to either party and two barbed wire gates twenty feet apart to open and close every time we visited them or vice versa. Since I had the onerous task of opening and closing said gates, I resented the needless duplication of effort.

Two years later my foster brother, George Clifford Wood, homesteaded the 640 acres adjoining our southern border. These statistics are based on the dates of consummation of the five-year "proving up" period required by law, not the filing dates.

Between Mosquito and Long Valley, Dave Swancott developed a fertile pocket of land into a prosperous dairy complete with Dutch windmill, a reminder of his native land. Unfortunately, his wife, Effie, did not share his love of the land and ran off with a traveling salesman.

When George was ready for high school, the family moved to Cedarville and opened a livery stable on Main Street, Lots 1, 2, 3, 4, and 9, 10, 11, and 12 of the Bonner Addition, District 2.[58] Today Lots 4 and 9 are Fire District, the rest are occupied by Page's Market, McClellans, Edward and Diane Cardona, and Joseph Gregory.

By 1920, Dad realized that horseless carriages had replaced the real thing and moved back to the ranch and bought the dairy herd that was subsequently lost to the rabies epidemic mentioned earlier.

CHAPTER 7

". . . I am driven on by the flesh;
and he must needs go that the devil drives."

All's Well That Ends Well, Act I, Scene III
William Shakespeare

On March 24, 1927, Case No. 2844, People *vs* Frank E. Page, came to trial in Alturas, California, and Dad and I were there. District Attorney Oscar Gibbons represented the People and A. K. Wylie and D. B. Robnett acted for the defendant, Judge F. M. Jamison presiding. The Jury included Foreman George Fordyce, Henry E. Smith, Herman W. Schadler, William Crow, Robert Cartright, Iva McGarva, R. B. Clark, Alfred L. Hays, Anna M. Frailey, David T. Garrett, R. D. Craig, and Fred M. Taylor. Witnesses for the prosecution were George T. Cline, licensed surveyor, who testified to the location on the map, People's exhibit 1, where the victim's body was found; medical examiner, Dr. Stiles; Coroner Frank E. Kerr; Sheriff John C. Sharp; garage man James C. Jarman; and Mrs. Mary Seminario who heard the screams, one big one and two little ones, July 6, 1926. The verdict was Guilty of Murder in the Second Degree and Page was sentenced to San Quentin for twenty years.[59] The trial lasted less than two days. I had hoped to see the defendant, Carey's father, but I was disappointed. He was seated in the front of the Court room with his back to me, and I was in the back row and not tall enough to see over the intervening crowd of adults. Still it was a learning experience in legal procedure for a seven-year-old.

Another act of violence that was not prosecuted occurred that summer. Dorris, Mother, and I were in the kitchen one day when we heard a dragging sound outside. It was Neil, crawling on his belly, his back a mass of dried blood and swollen flesh. As he lay face down on the floor, Mother and Dorris began the long, slow process of soaking loose the strips of blue chambray shirt that were embedded in the lacerations on his back. The pattern of parallel wounds suggested a cat-o-nine tails, but Neil was too weak from trauma and loss of blood to say much. He had tried to run away on horseback, but Uncle Ardie had overtaken him, beaten him, and left him for dead. We never knew how many days it took him to crawl to our place for help. It took hours to remove the shredded fabric, clean the damaged flesh, and apply Bag Balm to the injuries to prevent the bandages from sticking. Then we lifted him onto the cot, face down, until he recovered. When Dad saw Neil's condition, he said, "Tell Ardie the next time I see him, I'll kill him."

Ardie got the message. He sold his place to Forrest and Garnet Parry and dropped out of sight. Later we learned that he wound up in Los Angeles. At least we never saw him again.

When Neil recovered, we found him a new home where he could earn his board and room and attend school.

In late September, Dorris, Mother, and I made the stork run to Cedarville again. While we waited, I enrolled in the fourth grade. One day the teacher, Miss Brown, was ill so Mr. "Bud" Tyeryar, principal, substituted for her. The pupils were properly subdued. After all, his office was directly above our classroom and the sounds of corporal punishment, when administered, were clearly audible below. His first question spread panic. "Who had brushed his/her teeth that morning?"

Many of the children did not even own a toothbrush, let alone being conscientious about dental hygiene. As he called each name on the roster, he elicited an affirmative squeak. Alphabetically, my name was last and I had not brushed that morning. My toothbrush had been lost in the move to town. So when he thundered out my name, "Wood?" I said, "No," and waited for the heavens to fall. Instead, he said, "That's nothing. I haven't brushed mine in six months!" Honesty really is the best policy.

On September 20, 1927, Donna Lavine Wood arrived, the newest twig on the family tree, and we returned to Mosquito.

Without some background, some of the following incidents might seem irrelevant. When Oscar and Minnie Diessner and his elderly parents homesteaded the land across the valley from our place, Dad and Mother were pretty well established. New neighbors were always welcome and apparently all went well at first. But there is an old adage that says "Help a friend and make an enemy." Like most old adages, it endures because it is true. Dad was generous with his help, especially since Minnie was pregnant with her first child, and women in our culture were cosseted and protected during this "delicate" period. Unfortunately, "help" creates an imbalance of power in social relationships, unlike the fair exchange of goods and services which fosters a sense of equality. Oscar obviously resented his dependency on Dad's help and felt that wives were equal partners in a marriage and deserved no special treatment. When Minnie was harnessed up with their only horse to pull the plow, this difference of opinion erupted into a heated argument. Realizing that their continued commerce would only aggravate the situation, they declared an armistice and henceforth maintained a strict neutrality with minimum contact. Wisely they did not attempt to perpetuate their differences into a family feud. The Diessner girls and I were encouraged to be friends although our work schedules limited our association to the classroom.

Apparently, Oscar's "way" was right for them. When Minnie went into labor while pulling the plow, Oscar took her to the house where he delivered Amelia on the kitchen table and Minnie was given the rest of the day off. In fact, he delivered all six of their children, and I have never seen healthier people. Thanks to good genes and healthy diet, cottage cheese, rye bread, and sauerkraut, their hair shone, eyes sparkled, complexions bloomed, and teeth gleamed in friendly smiles. Besides good physical health, they enjoyed the security of family and a sense of achievement by contributing to the common goal.

Since they operated a Grade B dairy, they sold their butter fat and did not clog their own arteries with cholesterol. From the skim milk, they made cottage cheese which was shaped into patties like hamburgers and then dried on burlap "shelves" so air could circulate and expedite the drying process. During the school year, these patties were "reactivated" by a little skim milk and placed between slices of rye bread to make sandwiches for school lunches. To young appetites enhanced by physical labor, this fare was ambrosia for the gods. As I recall, Oscar did indulge himself with black coffee, but I never saw any evidence of sugar on the premises.

In every dairy, a herd bull is a necessary adjunct and is usually segregated from the cows, unlike range stock where breeding records are not kept. The Diessner bull was a mean-dispositioned Holstein. One day Oscar's father, doddering with age but still trying to help, was attacked by the animal. Only the courageous intervention of Nita, Border Collie bitch, saved the old man's life. She managed to sink her teeth into the bull's nose and to hang on until Oscar pulled his father to safety. Naturally, this act of heroism earned the dog a privileged place in the family hierarchy.

Whether it is true that dogs reflect their owners' personalities, certainly many people believe it. If so, Mr. Diessner had an ugly disposition. Both Nita and her mate, Carlos, would bite, with or without provocation, and leash laws did not extend to Mosquito Valley. However, there was usually a child available to restrain the dogs when the mail carrier delivered the mail to the Diessner Post Office on Mondays and Thursdays.

Since beginning teachers often start their careers in culturally deprived areas, our District usually rated the youngest and greenest. Miss Elsie Conners exemplified this credo. When George was transporting her from the train depot in Alturas to her new post in Mosquito, her reaction to the sight of a calf was, "Oh, look! A little cowlet!" George explained that the cowlet was really a bullet.

Obviously her inexperience was not limited to taxonomy but extended to class management problems as well. When the Diessner girls and I all denied responsibility for some minor infraction (I can't even remember what it was), Miss Conners declared that we would sit there until someone confessed. Since I had not done whatever it was, I suspected that the youngest girl, Bertha, had, but I also understood that the other girls, as members of the family, would not "rat" on one of their own. It did not occur to me at first that Miss Conners would extend this ultimatum beyond regular school hours, but she did. From the window by my desk, I could see storm clouds moving in from the south. If we didn't start home soon, we would be caught in a blizzard. Also, if we were late, parents would become concerned and come to see what was wrong. That would bring Dad and Mr. Diessner together in a confrontational situation, both honor bound to defend his own. With the "bad blood" already between them, I believed that that potentially explosive circumstance should be avoided at all cost, so I said, "I did it. Let's go home."

Miss Conners savored her empty triumph until we got about halfway home in the one-horse chaise that we used for transport in bad weather.

"Now, I want you to tell your folks the truth when we get home," she said.

"I will," I agreed. "I didn't do it."

"But you said you did!" she countered.

I didn't try to explain why I lied. I was anticipating my punishment for lying, the ultimate sin in Dad's book. According to him, the most heinous crime was made worse by lying about it, and while he had never specified the penalty, he had warned me that lying was the only thing for which he would punish me. Until now, I'd had nothing to worry about. Telling the truth came naturally.

When the horse was unharnessed and stabled, we entered the house and Miss Conners told her story and then I explained why I had lied. Miss Conners was dismayed to learn how closely her short-sighted edict had come to precipitating "real" trouble and apologized profusely. I was not punished for my "peace-keeping" lie.

In fact, I was rewarded. When I returned to school the following week, I was showered with favors and hand-made gifts. My "lie" had spared one of my classmates from punishment at home. In those days, punishment at school was reinforced by punishment at home.

Whether this incident led to the formal invitation to dine at the Diessner residence, when school was out, I still don't know. The folks and I debated the politics of accepting this gesture of good-will before penning a formal reply to the *Respondez, s'il vous plait.*

On the appointed day and hour, I arrived on the Diessner doorstep with some trepidation. While I now knew which fork to use at table, I wasn't as confident of my ambassadorial skills. Mrs. Diessner met me at the door, perspiring profusely. Preparing dinner on a wood stove in summer while six months pregnant will activate the sweat glands if anything will. When she showed me to the table, I was dismayed. Instead of the family-style setting that I expected, it was set for two, with the best china and flatware. Soon after I was seated, Mr. Diessner came in followed by Nita. He greeted me formally and sat down opposite me. The dog lay down under the table where she snapped at my feet all during the meal. Mrs. Diessner served fricasseed chicken and several side dishes of vegetables. I had hoped that my host would clarify the purpose of our meeting, but he only made small talk. I minded my manners and heaved a sigh of relief when it was over. I thanked them and left. The girls never showed themselves during my visit, and Minnie was only present as a servant. I'm sure that I was meant to feel honored but I only felt uncomfortable.

Although I always tried to follow the conditions in Kipling's poem, "If," in one instance I failed miserably. I was visiting George and Dorris. He was washing the car and two-year-old Georgie was "launching" chips on the surface of the water tank. As I watched, she stretched too far and tipped into the water head first. I tried to rush to her rescue but my feet ware rooted to the ground. I opened my mouth to yell at George but no sound came out. She was coming up for the third time when George looked up.

Instantly he fished her out, held her up by the heels, and slapped the water from her lungs. As he carried her dripping wet into the house, he said to me, "Why didn't you . . . ?" He must have seen the truth in my eyes and stopped. He handed Georgie to her mother and said, "She needs dry clothes. She fell into the tank." Nothing was ever said about my "freezing" in a crisis, and Georgie survived her experience without any fear of the water. George kept my secret, and I never "froze" again.

Since Mother continued to ignore the doctor's orders about dieting, he suggested that a change of scenery might help her to avoid food and thus prolong her life. Plans were made to visit Dad's oldest brother, Frank, in Plains, Montana. We loaded up our open touring car and headed north. I occupied the back seat and sulked. Travel held no interest for me. Exploration of the known universe could be more comfortably and economically achieved between the covers of a book and was not limited to the present. In books, there were no border inspection stations, authorized to strip, search and seize produce or unidentified flying insects that might have hitched a ride in an open vehicle. In reality, the "bug" station staff bottled up a couple innocent specimens, retired victoriously to their office, and left us to repack and reload our gear.

In books, we can pursue our journey without delays, detours, dead-ends, inconvenience, invasion of privacy, road work, motion sickness, jet lag, passports, inoculations, Montezuma's revenge, *ad infinitum.*

But for some reason, most people seem to enjoy being hung up in traffic, while the engines overheat, radiators boil over, carburetors develop vapor locks, and fan belts wear out. But who can resist the open road, a graveled one-lane trail, with turn-outs, that shake loose wires and hoses and chews up tires? Add sunburn, bug bites, and tedium at thirty miles an hour. Man, that's livin'! And you can brag to your friends back home (if you make it) about your wonderful vacation.

While I love the outdoors for work or play, I have zero tolerance for bugs or dirt in my food or in my bed. Therefore, I opt for the comfort and cleanliness of eating and sleeping indoors. As far as I am concerned, "sleeping rough" is a function of necessity not choice.

In spite of the hardships, we arrived in Klamath Falls, Oregon, in time for the Fourth of July celebration, which included rodeo, carnival, and horse racing. I was fascinated by the motorcyclists defying the law of gravity inside a steel-girded sphere. Since Dad had demonstrated centripetal force years before using a pail of milk, I understood the principle governing the cyclist's ability to ride upside-down. However, understanding how it was done did not diminish my appreciation of their skill and courage.

Later, in the bleachers, Dad confounded the spectators seated near us by accurately predicting the winners of each race. They were further confounded to learn that he did not use his "gift" to bet on the races. Before the final race, two men seated behind us got up to go place a bet on the favorite. Dad said, "Save your money."

"But," argued the men, "look at his record, the odds, etc. . . . ."

"He won't finish the race," said Dad.

They were still arguing when the race started. The favorite made a strong start and was leading the field when he fell, injuring both horse and rider. The men left, shaking their heads.

While in Klamath Falls, we visited Alex and Daisy Weilmunster, former residents of Long Valley. They laughingly told us that they were "living in sin." Their relationship had been tumultuous, resulting in frequent divorces and remarriages to each other. On their sixth or seventh visit to the Judge, he refused to perform another marriage ceremony "as a waste of time." Instead he told them "to go and live in sin and save divorce costs."

Since George's ex-wife and son also lived in Klamath Falls, we stopped by for a brief visit. I had never seen my four-year-old nephew, Donald, before, nor his mother, Uinta, either. Her new husband, Jack Caldwell, was a gracious host and smoothed over an otherwise awkward situation.

At that time, The Altamont district in Klamath Falls was primarily undeveloped swampland, but lots were being offered for $25.00 each. Dad saw the potential for residential development and wanted to invest several thousand dollars in the property, but Mother refused to sign the necessary papers. Whatever Dad wanted, she opposed on general principles. He even had to register as "Declined to state" on the voter rolls so that she couldn't learn his political preference and "kill his vote."

En route to Burns, Oregon, we stopped at another campground. While I sat in the back of the car being homesick, I was approached by a little girl with a tiny puppy, a Fox-terrier and Spitz mix. She offered to sell it for a penny. The transaction was completed in seconds and I had a companion. Then the folks returned to the car. Dad explained that we couldn't keep the dog. Hotels and motels did not allow pets. The puppy was returned and my penny recovered, but I was unhappy. Another camper, a woman in her thirties, saw me crying and asked me why. After I explained, she located Dad and chewed him out for depriving me of the puppy. To make a long story short, the puppy was restored to my arms and the penny to the little girl's pocket. Of course, our next stop at a Burns hotel confirmed what Dad had anticipated. There was no room in the inn for pets. I offered to sleep in the car with Tudy, but Dad solved the problem by smuggling her into the hotel room in his pocket (she was that small).

At Umatilla, Oregon, we crossed the Columbia River on a car ferry. I was amazed at the hollyhocks, which were taller than the buildings.

In Spokane, Washington, the folks renewed their acquaintance with the Kyle family. Their son, Russell, was about my age and we managed to strip a black cherry tree of its fruit while the adults reminisced. No one who has never experienced the delectable flavor and texture of a tree or field ripened fruit can appreciate the difference between today's hard, picked green, tough-skinned product and the real thing. Naturally, I had been familiar with Bings and Royal Anns, but undoubtedly the black variety was the non-pariel of the cherry family.

After Spokane, we headed east to Coeur d'Alene, Idaho, Thompson Falls, and Plains. Having spent most of his life on crutches, Uncle Frank had developed the physique of an athlete, his shoulders so wide that he had to angle his way through doorways. Aunt Edna was a diminutive person with a wry neck. Between them they had produced four fine strapping sons: Warren, Bruce, Marshall, and Victor. Only Victor was still at home and employed in the family business, commercial wood products, when we visited them. I helped Victor by stacking stove wood as he split it. When we left, Uncle Frank gave me a wooden puzzle that he had carved himself. With a little promotion, it could have been a commercial success.

Then we headed home, the only direction that made me happy. I was born with flat feet, not itchy feet.

CHAPTER 8

". . . Fair encounter
Of two most rare affections!
Heavens rain grace
On that which breeds between them!"

> *The Tempest*, Act III, Scene I
> William Shakespeare

We arrived home in time to attend a Box Social and dance at the Vya school house. This traditional event was the highlight of the season. Women exercised their ingenuity in creating the fanciest boxes imaginable, containing supper for two, and the lady's name concealed inside. These boxes were displayed on a table in front of the band stand. At midnight, the bidding by the men began. Even spouses did not know which box was which, so the auction generated considerable surprise, mirth, and camaraderie as the men opened the boxes and discovered the identities of their supper partners. The proceeds of the auction paid the musicians, usually Johnny Perry with the accordion, Dad on the violin, and Mrs. Perry or Theresa Perry at the piano. In those days, dances were major events. They started as soon as people could finish their evening chores and drive or ride to the hall. Once begun, they lasted until the sun came up, so the revelers could go home by daylight. No alcohol was allowed. Two bouncers, whose keen noses would put a breathalyzer to shame, manned the entrance, in case someone tried to violate the rules. Variety characterized the dancing: Polka, Schottische, waltz, fox-trot, square and round-dancing. Mother was official caller for the square dances. Although the clergy considered the waltz indecent "because of the physical proximity of the partners,"[60] Dad had taught me to waltz, which became my specialty.

However, the main event for me occurred before the dance started. While the band was tuning up, the gas lanterns were being pumped up, and the floor being sprinkled with soap-like flakes to increase its polish, the kids were running in and out of the building as kids will. I was standing beside the door when several of them burst through it, the edge of the door banging into my forehead. As I stood there dazed, a ten-year-old boy leaned forward and kissed the bump. There was instant bonding, a mutual, total commitment, like Siamese twins, who had been separated at birth and suddenly reunited. Instead of the Untouchables, we became the Inseparables. We went hand-in-hand, sat side by side, and shared the same desk in class. Boyd was a blond, raw-boned boy, son of Lawrence and Geneva Herrin. Lawrence was a rancher and road crew boss and Geneva was teacher and postmaster. Boyd's maternal grandparents, Mr. and Mrs. Jesse Strotts, operated a hotel and barbershop in Cedarville.

In retrospect, the most important aspect of these social occasions was the inclusion of whole families, no matter how young or old. Pallets were arranged along the edge of the bandstand for infants and toddlers to sleep on when drowsiness overcame excitement. No one was left home with a baby-sitter. It was togetherness at its best.

Not long after that, it became apparent that the Mosquito school District lacked funding for a teacher, so Dad sold the sheep to Mitchell Urells, and we moved to Vya for the school year, where I enrolled in the sixth grade. Students included Harry Eugene (Gene) Rose, Boyd Herrin, Carey Kemble, Margaret Mason, and yours truly. Vya was too far for the Diessner girls to commute and moving wasn't practical for the whole family.

On my ninth birthday, Mother baked a cake and Gene and Boyd pooled their resources to buy an Eva and Topsy set of dolls for me. I never played with dolls much, having live nieces to care for, but it's the thought that counts. I remember one Christmas when I asked for a steel erector set like Leland Harriman had. Santa delivered nineteen dolls of various sizes and shapes. Except for the largest, with a composition head and cloth body, which I operated on for Blue Blood and carefully sutured the incisions afterward, none was ever touched. Santa did better the next Christmas bringing me a friction train, a marvelous toy. However, the only gift that survives today is the book, *Recitations for Every Occasion*, that George gave me on my sixth birthday.

After Gene and Boyd had polished off the birthday cake and left, I tackled another issue with Mother. In exchange for no more spankings, I would make a special effort not to aggravate her any more. At 108 pounds

I was too big to spank anyway. Knowing that I could always go to Dad with my grievances, she acquiesced. She never spanked me again but she still hit me with her fist or threw dishes or stove-wood at me. Once she threw a glass which narrowly missed me and shattered above Georgie's head. That scared her into more rational behavior for a while.

At ten, Boyd was already driving the family car, a blue Chevrolet sedan, and he started teaching me how to drive. On one such occasion, I was behind the wheel, Boyd was beside me, and Gene was in the back seat. As I started to cross a small ditch, I tried to shift down to second gear but hit reverse instead, stalling the motor. Instantly, I felt a knife blade against my throat, Gene's typical reaction to stress. Quietly Boyd said, "Put it away, Gene." After a life time, Gene complied, and we continued my driving lesson. From the time Gene was four years old, when Mother baby-sat for his mother, a knife had been his security blanket and "equalizer."

On another occasion he threatened Boyd with a .22 rifle, but Boyd faced him down until Gene lowered the gun. Apparently this reliance on weapons reflected a deep-seated insecurity.

The Presidential election that fall featured Herbert Hoover, Republican, against Al Smith, Democrat. Since one of the functions of the school house was to serve as a polling place for voters, the kids had an unscheduled holiday.

Before the school year was out, we got the devastating news that fire had wiped out our ranch. Dorris had dumped some ashes from their wood stove outside. The ashes still had live embers. A south wind did the rest, blowing sparks into the neighboring brush. The resulting conflagration left nothing but scorched earth in its wake. Dad sold the land to Harry Wimer for three thousand dollars for sheep pasture.

When school was out, Dad traded the old Ford in on a Chrysler sedan with a large trunk-like box attached to the rear. One side of the box could be lowered to form a table in front of a cupboard containing food and utensils. Then we invited Lola and Maxine Hill to join us on a trip up to Smith River, California, to visit Ben and Stella Harriman and family, former Long Valley residents and neighbors. The three adults rode in front, while Packy and I and the dog shared the back seat with bedding and clothes.

We took highway 299 south to Red Bluff, then west on 36 to Forest Glen, California, a campground on the Mad River. Access to the camp was down a winding grade, one-lane wide with turn-outs and frequent signs reminding motorists to sound horn on every turn. However, sounding the horn did not prevent a head-on collision between our car and another large vehicle coming up the hill. The horns probably canceled each other out. In any event, the resulting damage to the steering apparatus on the Chrysler necessitated a two-week layover while waiting for parts. Packy and I were allowed to wade in the shallow edges of the river but were warned about the swift current in the middle of the stream and the falls immediately below the camp which had claimed many victims. Inevitably, we ventured beyond the safe zone and were caught by the current. Neither of us could swim, but survival is a great motivator. We learned in a hurry.

To explain another phenomenon that I observed while there, a brief description of the environs is necessary. Parallel to the white picket fence which marked the perimeter of the camp was a road. One afternoon while lying on the grass, I looked through the pickets at the passing cars and discovered a new optical illusion. As the wheels passed the pickets, they "reversed" themselves. I couldn't believe my eyes at first, so I called Dad for confirmation. The same illusion occurs in automobile commercials on television, sans pickets, about thirty per cent of the time.

When the parts for the car finally arrived, repairs were made and we continued west to the coast, and north to Crescent City. Off shore was a World War I destroyer which was "open" to the public. Dad and I wanted to go aboard but Mother balked at riding to the ship in a rowboat and climbing up a rope ladder to the deck. Instead, I had to settle for a ride on a horse-drawn sledge in the surf, a tourist attraction provided by a local entrepreneur of native American persuasion. He also warned us not to eat mussels harvested above the water line. We weren't interested in mussels anyway, but we did spend some time fishing off the high rocks for ling cod and "squaw fish," the latter leaving a silvery con-trail of glittering baby fish behind as the parent fish were pulled from the sea.

From Crescent City, we proceeded to Smith River where the Harrimans now lived. They had a son, Leland, and two daughters, Evelyn "Rosebud" and Dorothy. Mr. Harriman had recently undergone cancer surgery at the Mayo Institute in Rochester, Minnesota, to remove half of his lower jaw bone. Because this type of surgery was still in the experimental stage, the doctors operated for free.

While we were there, Rosebud and I went exploring the neighboring country side. Suddenly, she exclaimed, "Oh, a kitty!" "No, that's a skunk," I corrected her. The animal seemed to be struggling to escape some hidden trap. I went to the rescue. Its feet were stuck in what appeared to be tar smeared on a board or metal plate. I tried to calm its fear with soft talk, but obviously there was a communication gap. Finally I removed my hat and placed it over the struggling animal to limit the field of spray while I endeavored to pull its feet loose from the viscous snare. The skunk escaped, but my hat and I did not. The hat had been designed as a shade to keep the sun off my face so I wouldn't freckle, not as a gas mask. Hat and clothes were burned and I spent three days in the river before I was de-skunked. Even my dog kept her distance and whined in commiseration. As soon as I was fit to travel, we hit the road back to Cedarville.

It was evening in late July when we arrived at our destination. We stopped at the Polly Ann Bakery operated by the Koenig brothers, for coffee and doughnuts before retiring to our hotel room for the night. Mr. Koenig came forward, not to take our order, but to offer condolences. Donna, my favorite niece, had died a few days earlier from blood poisoning following a neglected black widow spider bite. I grieved, but Tudy was always there to lick away the tears.

Within a few days we were on the road again. Like the boll weevil, "We were lookin' for a home." Since any place away from Boyd was equally bad, I did not participate in the decision. Mother wanted to relocate in Chico so we did. Dad leased a two-story rental property, four apartments upstairs, next door to the Notwell Grocery Store. In the yard were two fig trees, one persimmon, and pomegranates along the fence.

When school started, I entered the seventh grade. Classes averaged twenty-five to thirty students with a total enrollment of about seven hundred. Quite a switch from the one-room schools that I had attended previously. Being a book worm I soon found myself on the Honor Roll which I thought was great until I learned that Honor Roll meant weekly presentations every Friday afternoon in the auditorium before the entire student body! I was petrified with stage fright. Guess I survived or I wouldn't be writing this memoir.

Since the stock market collapsed that fall, times were hard. One of the apartments was rented to a man whose wife had run off with another man leaving him with five small children to support picking prunes on a piece-work basis. Honest pay for honest work but hardly adequate to meet the needs of his family. Soon his rent was delinquent and Dad was sneaking groceries up the back stairs to augment their meager food supply.

Equally economically challenged were two women who traded some of their clothing for rent. It was quality attire, left over from better times which Mother converted into school clothes for me.

Although the circumstances differed, all of the tenants were poverty-stricken and welfare was just another word in the Preamble—not a social program. By Christmas, we were broke, too.

Again we loaded up our household goods and headed for Nevada. Julia, a lovely sixteen-year-old girl, also on her uppers, wanted to join our party. Naturally we couldn't refuse. She offered to spell Dad behind the wheel so she was driving up Burney Mountain when the steering mechanism fell apart and she lost control of the vehicle. After weaving back and forth between sheer drop-offs on the right and solid rock on the left, the car finally rolled over in the borrow pit. We climbed out, uninjured except for Dad who burned his leg on the exhaust pipe. The car was tipped back on its wheels and towed to a nearby campground to await new parts. Julia changed her mind about pioneering in Nevada and caught a ride back to civilization.

Eventually we made it to Vya. The Herrins told us that the Marriettes had separated and Layton had moved to Lakeview, Oregon, as a sales rep for the Zanol Company of Cincinnati, Ohio.[61] Therefore the former trading post was empty. It was good housing with a well and windmill, so we took possession. Being stranded in midwinter without fuel was a problem, but the surrounding sagebrush needed clearing anyway. I pulled up the brush from the snow, piled it crosswise on a horseshoe shaped loop of rope, and then pulled the loose ends over the wood and through the loop end, tightened it, and slung the load over my shoulder. Since brush burns quickly, it took about fifteen loads daily to keep the home fires burning. Sometimes Boyd would ride up from Vya on his horse, Peanuts, and help me gather fuel and to make plans for the future.

As I had to venture further afield each day to look for wood, I was a long way from home when I discovered a newborn calf frozen in the ice. Apparently the cow had dropped him there and while she was cleaning him up, his body heat melted the ice and he became embedded and unable to get up and follow her. I dug him loose and carried him home. We named him Lucky and later sold him to Carey for $6.00.

About this time, Chet Colvin appeared on the scene. He was a large man, probably six foot six, with hands like hams. While he did not distill illegal spirits himself, he provided transport and marketing for those who did. He wanted to rent a room from us. Since money was scarce, we agreed. At the time, our only income was the dollar twenty-five a week that I earned by washing shirts, two-bits each, for Lloyd Lycurgis "Pat" Heard, one of Herrin's road crew. Since Herrin was now in charge of over two hundred miles of highway in Washoe County, he was the heart of the job market.

Having recently been arrested and fined $200.00 for possession of ten gallons of Jackass,[62] Chet wanted a base of operations in Nevada, where only the federal "prohies" enforced the dry law.

Between Chet's rosy promises of bootleg profits and Mother's nagging about his failure as a provider, Dad decided to join the moon-shining fraternity. Chet advanced the price of grain, malt, and sugar. An old copper wash boiler was converted into a cooker, bread dough sealing the seams around the lid and the joint where the coil was connected to the center of the lid. As the distillate issued from the coil, it was captured in bottles, tested, and colored.

However, it was short-lived venture, two or three runs at most. As Dad said, he couldn't sell it to his friends, and he had no enemies. Until this lapse in lifelong respectability, alcohol had never been allowed on the premises, except for the watered brandy used as a non-allergenic substitute for milk in George's infancy, and vanilla flavoring.

Aside from the unprofitability of the enterprise, it also attracted undesirables. One such character was Frank Lorenzano, half-breed Indian, who later attacked E. R. Boston, Constable, in a drunken fight in Cedarville, was arrested and given a floater when he was released from jail.[63]

Frank was only one of several guests at our house one evening, but he was the only one who became obnoxious, aggressive, profane, licentious. Pat Heard, teetotaler, reminded him that there were ladies and minors present. Frank immediately became belligerent and challenged Pat to stop him. Pat, slight of build, fair complexioned, and fastidious, said, "Okay. Outside." Frank was taller and heavier than Pat and certainly more experienced in barroom brawls. He was also a poor judge of character. Frank went outside first and as Pat opened the door to follow him, Frank threw a heavy iron pump handle at his silhouetted figure. Only healthy reflexes saved Pat from being killed on the spot as the impromptu weapon crashed into the wall behind him. Pat grabbed the axe beside the door and advanced toward Frank who was keeping the water trough between them. But Pat wasn't playing games. He jumped up on the edge of the trough opposite Frank and swung the axe. Frank broke and ran, Pat in hot pursuit.

As bulky as he was, Frank slid between the rails of the pole corral like a greased pig and kept going. He was still running when the sound of his footsteps faded away in the distance.

CHAPTER 9

"All places that the eye of heaven visits
Are to a wise man ports and happy havens,
Teach thy necessity to reason thus;
There is no virtue like necessity."

King Richard II, Act I, Scene III
William Shakespeare

As if the depression wasn't bad enough with ten and a half million able-bodied men unemployed, conditions were worsened by drought in the midwest, both man-made disasters: the first by short-sighted monetary practices and the second by greedy exploitation of natural resources. By killing off most of the buffalo (pardon me, bison), and plowing up the plains in the windiest section of the country, wind and water erosion was inevitable and the first dry weather cycle left a dust bowl where buffalo once grazed in knee-deep forage. It shouldn't take a rocket scientist to realize that strip mining, clear cutting of timber, and exposing the topsoil to the elements can only compound the damage to our biosphere.

Given the straightened economic conditions, people resorted to various methods of survival. One such activity was rounding up wild horses for chicken feed. Because the former trading post provided the necessary corrals, chutes, and barns for such purposes, the process of culling out the older animals for chicken feed, gelding the colts, branding the mavericks, and selecting the cream of the crop to be "broken" for personal use, was conducted at our place. Sometimes, the more recalcitrant animals were added to Harry Wilson's bucking string for rodeos. One of these potential stars of the rodeo arena was a hammer-headed gray. To test his star quality, various cowboys tried to ride him, after working hours. He knew all the tricks and "dumped" them as fast as they got on his back. But one of the riders, Bill McCloskey, did not participate in the fun and games. He perched

71

on the top rail of the corral and watched as I did. After the other men left, Bill climbed down from his perch, cut out the big gray from the herd, and took up a position in the middle of the corral. At first, the frightened animal ran around him in circles. After a few minutes, Bill said in a soft drawl, "Naow, Silver, now, Silver." Gradually, the horse slowed, from a run to a trot, then to a walk. Bill continued crooning, "Naow, Silver," to the horse until it came to a stop, although it was still trembling. Then slowly Bill moved toward the "outlaw" horse and placed his hand on its withers. The trembling stopped as Bill stroked the animal, rubbing the sweaty hide from head to hoof. He examined the horse's hooves, checked his teeth, groomed his mane and tail, and crawled under him as if he were a pet. Then Bill started walking around the corral. Silver followed, first at a walk, then a trot, and finally a gallop. After that demonstration of "follow the leader," Bill mounted the horse bareback, guiding Silver with light pressure on his neck or sides. Next came the saddle and bridle and Bill on his back. Under his rider's gentle guidance, the horse performed perfectly. What a pleasure to see a horse "gentled" instead of "broken."

Having proved what kindness can do, Bill returned Silver to the herd, most of which were released to the wilds the following morning.

Another neighbor, John Harriman, had selected a chesnut sorrel, with a blaze face and four white socks, as his "share" for helping with the round-up. A few days later, he rode over to our place, leading his new horse, saddled and bridled, to condition it to the trappings of servitude. We agreed that he was a real beauty, but Dad said, "You'll never ride him, John."

"But he's not mean," protested John.

"Never said he was," responded Dad and changed the subject.

As expected, John's next visit confirmed Dad's prediction. The first time John mounted up, the animal reared, went over backward, and struck its head on a rock, killing itself.

While Dad had an uncanny ability to predict equine behavior, he did fairly well in the *homo sapiens* category as well. However, he maintained that any intelligent person could predict the future as well as Nostradamus. If history teaches us anything, it is that conditions tend to be cyclical in nature: climate alternates between wet and dry periods; the economy between boom and bust; political isostasy between war and peace; the cultural pendulum between Camelot and Sodom and Gomorrah. Taking these fluctuations into account and factoring in the constant of change one can make an educated guess concerning future events. Before social evolution replaced the Darwinian principle of the survival of the fittest, the trend was for the better. Now the natural process has been reversed. But, this, too, shall pass. Going against nature has always reaped its just desserts.

That summer, the school house at Vya was moved on skids to a new location about six miles north to better accommodate the student population. When school started, I was in the eighth grade and the "half-pupil" was six-year-old Jackie T. who was boarding with the Herrins. His mother, Dorothy, was one of the "girls" at a "house of ill-repute" at the State line between Nevada and California. Billie Day was the Madam of the establishment, as well as owner of a sand and gravel pit with which she supplemented her income from legal prostitution. She charged twenty-five cents per load for gravel.[64]

Formerly known as Reederville, the notorious speakeasy was now known as "Little Reno." The owners of the property were Pat Heard and Sam Painter.[65]

Aside from being a source of ardent spirits and other entertainment, it was also the only oasis for thirsty radiators between '49 and Cedarville. While motorists usually carried an emergency jug of water, they were not above stopping at "Little Reno" for a fill-up. One day, Dad, Mother, and I stopped and talked to Billie. Like many fat women, she had a strikingly pretty face. Also remarkable were her two neutered tom-cats, as big as bobcats and nearly the same color.

When we got home, I made a sketch of Billie from memory. The next time that we went to town, Dad insisted on showing my sketch to Billie. She wanted to buy it, but I gave it to her instead. Then she asked if we would be offended if she gave us some used clothing they had cleaned out of their closets. The discards were made of fine materials, and Mother made my eighth grade graduation dress from a pair of lavender crepe-de-chine lounging pajamas. The shoes fit me and learning to wear heels seemed to come naturally.

On July 15, 1931, George Wood, Constable of Long Valley Township, was called to Alkali Lake where Luther Hotho, eleven-year-old son of Mr. and Mrs. Fred Hotho of Roseville, California, allegedly shot himself with a 25-35 rifle. His cousin, fourteen-year-old Gene Rose, rode twenty-two miles to Harry Wilson's camp for help.[66] When investigating officers measured the victim's arm length and the length of the gun barrel, they concluded that it was physically impossible for Luther to have pulled the trigger, but there was no evidence that it wasn't an accident.

In September, Frank Estes, recently arrested by George Wood, Constable, on a complaint by Tom Dufferena, for grand theft of wire from sheep corrals at Badger Flat, was tried and found guilty *in absentia* by Justice of the Peace Albert Kemble.[67]

Also making news was the fire at "Little Reno" which consumed the buildings and forced the tenants to relocate.[68]

Then appendicitis claimed another victim. When Phyllis Dolores Stanley, six-year-old daughter of Fred and Lucille Stanley, became ill, Dr. Kennedy was called. He urged immediate surgery but Lucille wouldn't give consent without "Fed" (she lisped) and Fred was working at Hanging Rock. By the time Fred arrived, it was too late.[69]

In November, "Slim" a.k.a. Chet Colvin, Nevada's bootleg king, slipped off the grade near the Raymond Turner ranch in Cedar Pass. He was pulled out and arrested by Deputy Ray Tierney for possession of alcohol and carrying a concealed weapon.[70] The weapon was a derringer, a short-barreled pocket pistol of large caliber, which Chet habitually carried.

When Mother was cleaning out his room after his arrest, she called me to come see what she had found. As I entered, she opened a small notebook and showed me a revolting sketch of sodomy. I retched and fled.

That winter was a hard one, snow drifted so deep in '49 canyon that the snow plow had to tunnel a road through. The mail carrier rode a horse from Cedarville to '49 and then went on snowshoes the remaining three and a half miles to Vya.

Although I had completed eighth grade, I was still too young to enter high school, so we spent the intervening year at '49, former trading post on the '49 trail. It was a two-story structure, the upper floor designed to accommodate the transient population overnight. A wide, covered porch along the front welcomed tired travelers. The upstairs walls had been lined with burlap and calcimined white. I soon discovered that it was an excellent surface for etching, using a nail instead of a stylus. Because of a chemical reaction between the burlap and white wash, the lines were all pink.

The former barns and stables had been converted to lambing and shearing sheds for the sheepmen.

A mile or so west of '49 were the ruins of the Feight roadhouse where H. E. Cochran shot and killed the proprietor L. E. Feight, May 17, 1918.[71] The homicide followed a quarrel over one of the girls, Feight's daughter. According to Dad, Cochran wanted to make an "honest woman" of her and Feight objected, arguing that Cochran had no right to deprive him of his means of livelihood. In the ensuing gun fight, Cochran shot Feight five times, the bullets "pinning" him to the wall. Cochran turned himself in to authorities in Cedarville and was later exonerated in a Winnemucca, Nevada, court.

While the previous winter brought us deep snow, 1933 was characterized by the deep freeze. Temperatures dropped to -40-44 degrees Fahrenheit and the air "burned" our lungs. Since our central heating system was a wood heater in the living room, we lingered there as long as possible before retiring to our icy bedrooms. My bedroom was located in the southwest corner of the building with a window facing the road. As I started to undress one night, I saw the brim of one of those cow-pie caps extending beyond the edge of the gaping curtains. I pulled my dress down and returned to the living room where Dad was stoking the stove for the night. I reported what I had seen, and whereas he didn't doubt my veracity, he couldn't believe a peeping Tom would brave such cold. On the chance that I was not "seein' things," he went outside and fired a couple rifle shots into the air. We tried to find tracks but the full moon was directly overhead, casting no shadows on the frozen snow. Later, I heard the sound of hooves and saw a rider leading a pack burro gallop by.

When morning came, the footprints left by the visitor were clearly visible, confirming the presence of an uninvited guest who left Sasquatch-sized tracks behind. We followed his trail which showed where he had fallen once in his haste to get back to his horse and burro.

About the middle of February, 1933, George and Dorris stopped by on their way to Cedarville. Boyd was with them but we didn't have a chance to talk much before they left. When I asked him why he was going to town, he said that "he was full of poison" and held up his long bony hands for my inspection. In the lamp-light, I couldn't see that much difference from the norm and was more puzzled than alarmed.

A few nights later, we were again grouped around the heater, Dad and I reading and Mother sewing, when I looked up from my book and saw Dorris' face through the glass in the door. I said, "Boyd's going to die." When Dorris entered, she told us that Boyd was worse and they were taking his folks to town. For the next three days I neither ate nor slept, just grieved. Boyd died February 24, 1933, of tubercular meningitis.

For months afterward, I would "see" him when I was outside. He would come riding up to me on his horse, Peanuts, dismount, and start to put his arms around me, and then disappear.

75

As his friend, Orvis "Buck" Hill, so aptly wrote:

> *"The stem of the rose is broken*
> *Nipped in the bud of youth;*
> *So sudden was his departure*
> *It's hard to believe the truth."*

Spring brought the lambing season, followed by marking and docking, and shearing of adult sheep. But the big news, was that the industrial revolution had finally reached the very outposts of civilization! The sheep would be sheared by machine! I envisioned a box-like device which admitted a wooly ovine at one end and decanted a shorn product at the other. Imagine my disillusionment when I discovered that the "machine" was nothing but mechanized clippers similar to the ones used on me when I had my first haircut!

The shearing crew were Portuguese and Mexicans, who bunked upstairs during their sojourn at '49, rendering my "art studio" off limits until they left. Off limits for me but not Joe Rajas, who also liked to draw. When I reclaimed my atelier, the walls were solid murals.

Another thing that I observed was that sheep-shearers probably have the softest, whitest hands, next to movie stars, in the work force, and due to the same source: wool fat, or lanolin, key ingredient in ointments and cosmetics.

At '49, the outdoor "facilities" was located on the hillside some distance from the house. There was no door, but an inner partition screened the occupant from casual passers-by. Obviously the original builder did not factor in potential peeping toms. As I started through the doorway, I caught a peripheral glimpse of a large figure crouching behind a sagebrush and holding his sheep dog still to avoid detection. Naturally I reversed course and headed for the house. Realizing that he had been discovered, the man took off like a scalded cat, running so fast that his dog had difficulty keeping up. Of course, I recognized him. Because of his large size, he was called "Chiquita" and allowances were made for his limited abilities. His overgrown physique and small head suggested an excess of pituitary glandular secretion during his early development.

In any event, he either changed his ways, or his target. I never surprised him peeping again.

When fall came, we moved into the Bill Grobe house in Cedarville. William Grobe and Dr. M. R. Kennedy were proprietors of the Modoc

Silver Fox Farm, two miles south of town. The farm was started in 1926 and in 1929 they sold nineteen pelts at $150.00 to $200.00 each.[72]

I was one of 104 students enrolled that year. My teachers were Mrs. Hallie Tierney (later Superintendent), Mr. Smith, principal, Miss Muriel Worth, Miss Jesse Lee Stovall, and C. G. Guarneri. Because of my academic achievement, I was soon being excused from regular classes to work on posters for upcoming events or to finger-wave other girls' hair for the same reason. At that time, my hair was as straight as a string and equally attractive.

On September 29, 1933, Geraldine Marie (Gerry) Wood was born to George and Dorris Wood of Vya, Nevada, at the home of Mrs. Fred Hill in Cedarville.[73]

Although Mother was in no pain, her condition was deteriorating, accompanied by light seizures. To help control and enforce her diet, she was hospitalized temporarily, but she stole food from the other patients and was sent home. Dr. Kennedy said that the decision was up to the family. If she was kept in restraints, on a prescribed diet, she might live another two years. Without such a regimen, she would last two months, but she would die "full" and presumably happy. The decision was made to send her to Vya to live with George and his family.

As she was leaving, she walked by me and hit me with her fist. I said, "Why did you do that? I didn't do anything."

"No," she said, "You never do anything."

Two months later, Georgie came into the kitchen to find Grandma dead on the floor. George and Dorris were attending a movie in town when the emergency message was flashed on the screen.

It was an open casket funeral and as we filed by, I could see the faint bruises on her head where she had fallen. Otherwise, she looked at peace.

After that, Dad was gone, working somewhere, so I "batched" for the rest of the school year, often without food. If Nettie Hanks, our neighbor across the street, had not shared her meager meals with me, I would often have gone hungry. Her husband, Dan, was a World War I veteran who probably received a small pension. Gravy and biscuits require little but flour and meat drippings.

On May 26, 1934, I attended the home wedding of Herb Wood and Marcella Wheeler. George and Dorris were witnesses and Reverend Virgil A. Vinyard officiated. During the ceremony, I got the giggles when the bride and groom were solemnly swearing "to love, honor, and obey." It was common knowledge that they were already cohabiting and fighting like cats and dogs. While it is socially acceptable to weep at weddings, giggling is not, so I covered my face with my hands and "faked" the proper emotion.

After the ceremony, there was a reception, and guests began toasting the newlyweds. As these toasts grew more risque, George intervened, reminding the group that there were "ladies" present and nodding in my direction. The festivities continued, but the ribaldry did not.

One day as I was walking home from school, one of my neighbors stopped in his pick-up to offer me a lift home. Since he was a married man with three children, I tried to think of an excuse to decline without being rude but could not. Surely it was safe to ride the few blocks home. Of course, as soon as I was on board, he remembered an errand that he had to take care of before going home. He turned around and drove back downtown, through Main Street, and turned up Deep Creek canyon near the cemetery. The road crossed the creek part way up. While the water was not deep, it was prudent for drivers to proceed slowly to avoid splashing water on the spark plugs and stalling the motor. Apparently my neighbor did not slow down enough and the motor "died" midstream. He climbed out in the knee-deep water to dry the plugs and to restart the engine. This process proved time-consuming and frustrating. When the engine finally started, the man reversed the pick-up, turned, and drove directly home. Whatever his "errand," it was forgotten.

As soon as school was out, Dad and I moved to the Charles Sheldon National Wildlife Refuge in northern Nevada where he was employed as "powder man" for the fire tower foundation and to quarry the stone for the headquarters building.

In the late 1800's and early 1900's, the decreasing antelope populations of northwestern Nevada began to concern both residents and conservation groups. Through the efforts of the Boone and Crockett Club and the National Audubon Society, funds were raised and in 1918 the Last Chance Ranch (30,000 acres) was purchased from Jesse and True Hapgood.[74]

The Boone and Crockett Club, founded in December 1887, was the first club of its kind, dedicated to promote (1) manly sport with rifle; (2) travel and exploration; (3) preservation of our large game; (4) inquiry . . . and observation of natural history of wild animals and (5) interchange of opinions and ideas on the above. Theodore Roosevelt became the Club's first president.[75]

When Dad and I arrived at the Refuge, Ernest J. "Smiles" Greenwalt, former journalist, was manager. Also in residence were Mr. and Mrs. Floyd L. McTimmonds and their three children, Myrna, Erma, and Guy; Wallace Wood, two stone masons and two carpenters. Later the University of Nevada football team signed on for summer jobs of digging post holes and other labor-intensive tasks, thanks to the National Industrial Recovery Act which provided funding.

Water for the camp was piped from a nearby spring. Since the end of the pipe was elevated about six feet to accommodate the water trucks and other equipment, it created a continuous waterfall. The football players couldn't resist the temptation to shower and cavort in the icy water. Then they discovered that women lived there, too, much to their em'bare'ssment (sic).

Being young and justly proud of their physical prowess, they tended to brag. Finally, my cousin, Wally, said, "Why, my cousin, Maxine, can out-lift the whole bunch of you." I was somewhat nonplused by this challenge, but I couldn't let Wally down. The test was to lift one end of a granite slab that Dad had quarried. Each of the team members tried without success. I was unusually strong and had learned how to lift (press), so I was able to justify Wally's faith in my brawn. Fortunately, "showing off" is part of the maturation process and most people outgrow it.

One evening, Tudy came running into the tent and begged for water. Dad recognized strychnine poisoning and told me not to let her have any water. We had no raw eggs to force down her throat as an antidote, so we watched helplessly as she went into convulsions, and I was sure that she was dying. Gradually the seizures subsided and she lived. A few years later I observed another poisoned dog die instantly when he drank some water.

When fall arrived, we folded our tent and headed for Vya. Somewhere along the line, Dad had a drink or two, maybe celebrating the repeal of Prohibition. Being unused to strong spirits, it was enough to cloud his judgment. First, he and George got into a heated argument over who should pay for a grave marker for Mother's grave. George felt that it was Dad's responsibility as surviving spouse. Dad pointed out that George owed it to Mattie, that he had a good income. George said that he had a wife and kids to support. Dorris and I cleared the dinner table and went to the kitchen to do dishes. She washed and I dried. In the middle of the process, Dad burst into the kitchen, ordering me to, "Come on. We're leaving."

"Just a minute, 'til I finish drying the dishes." I said.

"No, now!" he roared and left. I thought that his behavior was unreasonable and finished drying the dishes. When I went outside, he was gone.

A few days later, George came home from work and said that Dad had decided to go back to South Dakota, and we would be taking him to the bus stop in Alturas the next day. We arrived early at the station, so we went to the Bridge Cafe for lunch. Their specialty was fried oysters, two or three of which covered a plate. I was reluctant to try them, having a poor opinion of the soup-sized variety, but George insisted that I at least try them. Talk about delicious! But like so many over-harvested species, today the *O.lurida* of the Pacific Coast is just a bite-sized shadow of its former self.

At the bus station, we said goodbye and promised to write. On our way back to Vya, we stopped in Cedarville to make inquiries about a possible placement for me to work while I continued my education. Mr. and Mrs. Warren Robinson owned and operated a chicken farm east of Cedarville, and Mrs. Robinson also taught school in Eagleville. They were looking for a board-and-roomer to help out. Being childless, they had adopted a little boy who was well on his way to becoming a spoiled brat.

My first instructions on the job were not to speak, not even to ask a question about my work, until all my chores were finished. My schedule started at 3:30 A.M. when I got up and went out to the three long chicken houses and started the heaters going. Then back to bed until 5:00 A.M. when it was time to prepare breakfast. After the meal, I washed the dishes and cleaned the house before walking a mile and a half to school. When I got home, I candled, weighed, and crated eggs until dinner time. After dinner, I worked until 9:00 P.M., when I was allowed to learn to type on their manual Remington typewriter. The keys were capped so that I couldn't "cheat." Although I had my own room, there were no locks on the doors, and Jackie regularly invaded my space, ransacking my belongings and messing up my homework. Naturally, I was not allowed to keep Tudy with me, so George and Dorris agreed to keep her for me at Vya.

After Christmas, a blizzard and wind storm struck Surprise Valley, uprooting the poplar trees along Main Street and blowing over a school bus taking children home to Eagleville. As a result, Principal Smith ordered all students who lived out of town not to attempt to go home. If they couldn't stay with friends, he would authorize rooms at the local hotel. I spent the night with Packy and her family.

By morning, the storm had blown itself out and snowdrifts blocked the roads and filled the lanes waist-deep with snow. I didn't wait for the roads to be plowed but waded back to the farm. I was soaked to my armpits by the time I reached the place. Apparently, Mrs. Robinson was prepared for my return. She opened the door and set my suitcase on the door-step. When I tried to explain why I had not returned the previous afternoon, she interrupted me. "I don't want to hear it. If I can't depend on you, you can't stay here," and slammed the door. So I picked up my suitcase and waded back to town. Then I canvassed the town, knocking on every door and asking if the household had any chores that I could do to earn my keep while I attended high school. Many people were sympathetic but couldn't help, until I came to the P. B. Harris residence. A lovely white-haired lady opened the door and listened to my story. She invited me in and showed me a room upstairs. Julia's hair had turned white prematurely when she was nineteen. Then she introduced me to her three young daughters, Joyce, Jimmie Lou, and Tatzie. Although she had a washing machine for the laundry, there was no machine for the ironing. Only long hours at the ironing board could keep all those ruffles, ribbons, bows, flounces, pleats, gathers, and shirring, standing at starched attention. Most of my time was spent ironing but I never saw the bottom of that clothes basket. Every day Julia added more clothes to the basket and I never managed to catch up, but between us we kept those little girls looking like princesses.

Their father, Percy Harris, was a successful businessman. Besides being an architect and contractor, he operated a lumber yard and car dealership.

A few weeks after I moved in with the Harris family, I received a letter from my former employer saying "not to be dramatic; that Mr. Smith had explained why (I) had not returned on time, so my job was waiting." For all I know, it may still be waiting.

In April, the Harris Lumber Yard got the Government contract for the construction of two CCC (Civilian Conservation Corps) camps in northern Washoe County, Nevada, one at Swinford Springs and the other at Board Corrals.[76] When Percy completed the specifications for the construction, I was given the opportunity to practice my typing skills on the contract. Thirteen copies were required and this was before photocopiers were invented. Mimeograph copies were not acceptable.

Little wonder that I developed a bone felon on the end of my left index finger. It took weeks of pain before it suppurated so that Dr. Kennedy could lance it. A few days later, Julia was changing the bandage when I suddenly felt too warm and headed out the door to the backyard.

"You're not going to faint, are you?" she called and I said, "I never have and I'm not going to start now." Famous last words. As I started to regain consciousness, I thought I was lying on a soft white bed, with the sun shining in a blue sky, birds singing, flowers blooming. Then I opened my eyes. I was lying on the ground among the dead weeds under an overcast sky. No sun, no birds, no flowers.

In the middle of May, George opened a pool hall and restaurant in the new building on the corner of Locust Grove and Main in Cedarville.[77]

One fine summer evening four of us, "X" and his future wife and my date and I, stopped at Koenig's Bakery for coffee and doughnuts before returning to our respective homes. "X" introduced the subject of committing the perfect crime, purely as an intellectual exercise, of course. Knowing that "X" had had some close encounters with the law, I rather doubted his objectivity. I took the position that the perfect crime was impossible because no one could control all the variables in a given situation, citing the Loeb-Leopold case as a concrete example. Nothing was settled but the discussion lasted longer than usual. As we left the Bakery to go our separate ways, "X" and I headed south. On our way, we passed a vacant building sometimes used as a bunkhouse by one of "X"'s in-laws when he came to town overnight. "X" said that he was going to check to see if "Y" was there. When he opened the door, he exclaimed, "Hey, com'ere. See what's in here." I approached cautiously and craned my neck to see the source of his excitement. Then he threw his arm around me, pulled me inside and tried to kiss me. I ducked my head to avoid the kiss and bit him on the shoulder. He hit me with his fist, knocking me down, flat on my back. Instantly, he was astraddle my mid-section. Time for Contingency Plan I.

"Let me up or I'll scream."

"Go ahead. Nobody'll hear you."

Since I was no better at screaming than at singing, I suspected that he was right. Plan II. I relaxed and said, "All right, but not here. "Y" might come. Let's go up to Lover's Lane." I had never been there, but I had a general idea where it was located, from hearsay. As we walked arm-in-arm toward our destination, I managed to take the long way around and to reach a particular street. About halfway along the street, I stopped.

"This is as far as I'm going," I said. "Wally lives here."

Like all men who resort to force to achieve their goals, "X" was basically a bully and a coward. He called me everything but a lady, being careful not to raise his voice, and strode off polluting the air with foul language. I stood there until I was sure that he was gone, then keeping to the shadows, I circled back to Main Street and crawled into the back seat of George's car to spend the rest of the night.

Fortunately, I have never had to go to Contingency Plan III.

CHAPTER 10

". . . . O, be some other name!
What's in a name? that which we call a rose,
By any other name would smell as sweet."

Romeo and Juliet, Act II, Scene II.
William Shakespeare

Also in May 1935, I received a letter from my maternal grandfather, Francis Fletcher Heald, telling me that he and my Uncle Wilbert Heald would be stopping by to see me on their trip from Oakland, California, to Seattle, Washington. I was ecstatic. At long last, I would learn the answers to all my family questions. After the introductions and before any meaningful dialogue could occur, Uncle Wilbert took me aside and said, "Don't mention your mother to Dad. He never allowed her name to be spoken after her disgrace." Hardly an auspicious beginning for acquiring the information that I wanted. Then Grandfather had his turn. "Don't mention your mother to Wilbert. We never talk about her." So much for great expectations! Actually, they probably didn't *know* anything after the "shotgun wedding" and the "never darken their door again" edict. My grandparents separated soon after, and grandfather moved to Stockton, California. Uncle Wilbert was a mail carrier in Oakland. While Grandmother apparently maintained a tenuous relationship with her banished daughter, she did not share her intelligence with the rest of the family. In fact, they had only recently learned that I existed.

While everyone agreed that my mother was a beautiful girl and that I was ugly, I bore enough resemblance to her to dispel any suspicion of imposture. Grandfather gave me a snapshot of his home in Stockton and one of my other uncle who was shell-shocked in World War I and spent his remaining days in a Veteran's hospital. He also brought a rare edition of a newspaper covering the assassination of President Lincoln. He left it with me to read, with instructions to return it when I finished, which I did.

On their way to Seattle, they stopped in Portland, Oregon, and secured a copy of my birth certificate for me, for which I was profoundly grateful. It only took another sixty years to learn that the information given for my father's place of birth was incorrect, but that's life.

As usual, deer hunting season took its toll of victims in accidental shootings. Johnnie Seminario, one of my classmates, and Monroe Dorton were killed that fall.[78]

Following basketball practice by the CCC boys from Swinford Springs, Coach Guarneri had closed the high school gym about 9:00 P.M. Around midnight, William Gooch saw flames at the high school and rushed to ring the fire bell, but Herb and Wallace Wood were already there.[79] The volunteer fire fighters responded nobly, but nothing was saved but a few desks. Even the records were destroyed.

Although the two-story brick structure was only thirty years old at the time of the fire, it had been condemned as unsafe. In 1903, the building had cost $10,500. At that time there were five teachers and Mr. Irving C. Raymond, principal. Trustees were Charles H. Lamb, president; William T. Cressler, clerk; H.B. Stevens, Wm. T. Strief, and Frank K. Powers.[80]

Two months after the fire, P.B. Harris submitted the low bid of $63,000 for construction of a new building.[81] Of course, work did not begin immediately. Classes were dispersed among several public buildings: the IOOF and Masonic Halls, and the old morgue for math and science because it had running water. I was volunteered to clean up the former mortuary, next door to Heath Stanley's newspaper office. The building had been vacant for years and never cleaned: sinks, counters, tables, and shelves were thick with grime. Thick, dark glass bottles with stoppers containing embalming ingredients, many with skull and crossbones, still lined the shelves. I could identify the more common pharmaceuticals like formaldehyde, alcohol, salts, and dyes but not all. Naturally, there was no refrigeration in those days. Cadavers had to be processed immediately. With lots of soap and elbow grease, the old morgue was soon converted from a relic of the dead to a shining classroom for the living.

After graduation in 1936, Raymond Hill, son of Mr. and Mrs. Ray Hill, left for Annapolis where he received appointment of Cadetship at the Military Academy.[82] During World War II, he was the youngest

Commanding Officer of a battleship, the *U.S. Nevada*, sunk at Pearl Harbor five years later.

On a visit to Long Valley that summer, Eva Henderson and I stopped by the Kemble place. While we were there, Eunice's six-year-old daughter, Josephine, was lying on a cot fussing, obviously ill. Her grandmother, Tiny G. decided that she needed a dose of castor oil and went to fetch the bottle and a tablespoon. Without even thinking, I said, "If she has appendicitis, castor oil is the worst thing to give her." Instantly Paul and EllenGrace, who were just leaving on a date, reacted with concern.

"Do you think she has appendicitis?" But they didn't wait for an answer. They bundled up Josephine and her mother and rushed off to the hospital, where the child had emergency surgery for appendicitis. This had been my first opportunity to square accounts with the elderly Paiute at Massacre Lake whose timely intervention probably saved my life.

No Surprise Valley Fair and Rodeo was complete without Mrs. Neva Lowell of Fort Bidwell. Her horse took first prize in the races.[83] She and her husband, Chester, operated a general mercantile store in Fort Bidwell, and he was the bank manager at the time of the "crash." He distributed $60,000 of his own money to local depositors who lost their money when the banks closed. Sure it was good P.R., but that was not his motivation. He was just that kind of guy.

That summer George and Dorris asked me to baby-sit Georgie and Gerry and to help out in the cafe, so I left the Harrises with some regrets, but family comes first.

Now that I was sixteen and officially old enough to date, Dorris told me that if a man asked me to go out with him, to refer him to her, which I did. She would tell him that I could only date non-drinkers. This restriction posed no problem. Even drinkers were willing to comply with the rule and to stay sober for the duration of our date. After she and George separated, I continued the practice of dating non-drinkers only. Alcohol distorts the perceptions and lowers inhibitions, resulting in objectionable behavior. The adverse effects of alcohol are demonstrated daily in crime, accidents, domestic violence, health problems and loss of productivity.

As it turned out, my job with George and Dorris was short-lived. By fall, their marriage was on the rocks, and I was sent back to South Dakota via Greyhound. Dad met me at the station, but he was financially unable to help me. At 63, he was receiving a pension of $19.00 per month. He subsisted on oats cereal without milk or sugar.

He took me to meet his sister, Aunt Annie Berryman, widow. She appeared to be an embittered old woman, somewhat short on the milk of human kindness. She owned an impressive residence and "let" rooms in better times. Although she had vacancies, she made it abundantly clear that my stay was temporary.

Early on, Uncle Bob took time off from his busy practice to show me the sights: Fort Meade, east of town; his cabin out of town; and the natural wonders: the Black Hills and the Badlands. Mount Rushmore was in the process of becoming a national monument.

Dad and I also visited Uncle Cal and his wife, Delilah, (nee Smith) and their nine children. Uncle Cal was a prominent farmer in the area and well able to provide work for an extra hand. Not only was I familiar with farm life, I was a fine healthy specimen of marriageable age and I was sitting across the table from four healthy young men who were in the market for a spouse. It didn't take a fortune teller to predict the future if I accepted their offer of board and room. However, I still had my heart set on an education, so I declined their offer. Naturally, they felt rejected and washed their hands of any further involvement with my problems.

Back in Sturgis, I canvassed the town looking for work to earn room and board, without any luck. In one poorer section of town, I met outright hostility.

"Get out!" shouted the women. "We need the money more than you do. We have children to feed!" At first, I didn't understand what they were talking about. Then I realized that they saw me as competition for the soldiers' "recreation" dollars. The women were trying to support their families by prostitution, at fifty cents a trick. I beat a hasty retreat.

Eventually, I was hired to keep house and to baby-sit two boys for a local photographer. All went well until one day the boys were playing outside and decided to knock down the large icicles hanging from the eaves. Unfortunately, one of the icicles fell against a large plate glass window, shattering it. In a fury, the man attacked the boys with a snow shovel and then fired me for negligence.

My next job was out of town on the Grubl farm. Paul Grubl was a well driller and his wife a former teacher. They had six children between the ages of four and thirteen, and her mother and two brothers, Mora and Roy Tibbits, lived in one wing of the house. Mrs. Grubl had to have surgery so I was hired to cook, keep house, and baby sit in her absence.

Bread-making was a daily necessity to feed a dozen people and to make school lunches. After Edith came home, I stayed on.

As if drought and depression are not enough to try men's souls, the temperature dropped to minus 44 degrees Fahrenheit for two weeks. The men bundled up like Eskimos to take out the slops and to tend the livestock. Within fifteen minutes their breath had congealed into icicles.

Then I heard about a job at Fort Meade. An officer and his wife wanted a baby-sitter and the pay was $.50 a day. Hurray! Now I could save up enough money to buy a ticket back to California! What was not explained in advance was that I had to rent a room in town, at, you guessed it, $.50 a day! But one good thing came out of my brief employment there. The officer gave me the address of the Navy Department to pursue my parent search. My letter of February 5, 1937, was referred to the Marine Corps, and within eight days I received the following reply:

"The records show that Charles H. Tendering was Honorably Discharged from the Marine Corps on August 26, 1922, at Mare Island, California, and further show that his death occurred on July 21, 1935, at El Centro, California."

I was a year and a half too late.

Finally, I found another job at $.50 a day where I could live-in. The new job was at a boarding house, but I was soon replaced by a needy relative of the manager.

However, the Browns, hotel managers, told me that I could stay in my former room for free, as long as no one else wanted to rent it, so, at least, I had a roof over my head. This situation continued for six weeks. Once a week, Mora Tibbits would come to town for the mail and supplies. He would stop by and take me to the cafe for doughnuts and coffee, my only food. My experience with fasting has been that hunger only lasts three days. After that, the appetite disappears and even the smell of food is nauseating. By the time Mora came by each week, the thought of food gagged me, but I choked down the doughnuts anyway, to survive. As soon as I ate, the food reactivated the hunger pangs for three days, followed by loss of appetite.

Whether Mora finally figured out the true state of affairs or not, he suggested that they could use my help out at the farm. I was delighted to go back.

Soon after I returned, the farmers started planting the spring crops. The government provided the seed. When the grain was two or three inches high, the wind would increase in velocity (it never stopped) and literally roll up the thin topsoil and sprouting grain like a carpet, exposing the bare rocks. The farmers would wait for more soil to blow in and then replant. This process occurred three times before I left in May to take a paying job with Mrs. Tobias, who operated a fried chicken cafe. I ironed, baby-sat two children, and prepared the frozen chickens for the deep fryer.

One payday, I drew my pay, said goodbye, and headed west. Besides the clothes on my back, I had $1.25, a comb and toothbrush. Sandals weren't designed for a two thousand mile trek, but that's all I had. Although thousands of mid-westerners were migrating to California, most rode the rails. Few resorted to hitch-hiking. In the four days that I was on the road, I never saw another hitch-hiker, but the trains which ran parallel to the highway were loaded with migrants, especially the open gondolas.

Out of Deadwood, two gentlemen of Jewish persuasion picked me up. When they learned that California was my destination, they started asking me about Hollywood and would not believe that I had never been there. My next hitch was a rancher in a truck who let me ride in the back as far as Newcastle, Wyoming. By then it was evening, and I hoped to sit in the lobby of a hotel until morning. The town Marshall told me that the lobby was off-limits, but I could sleep on one of the cots in the basement. At daylight, I was out on the street trying to orient myself when the Marshall appeared at my elbow. "Not going without your breakfast, are you?" he asked. He escorted me to a cafe and ordered eggs and hash-browns for me. Unfortunately, the eggs were sunny-side up and I couldn't have eaten them if my life depended upon it, but I relished the toast, potatoes, and coffee.

I thanked the Marshall and hit the road. Unlike many hitch-hikers, I never stopped and waited for a lift. I kept walking, every step taking me closer to California. Soon a traveling salesman with two black eyes stopped to offer me a lift.

After the salesman dropped me off, two men in a pick-up stopped and asked me if I wanted a ride. They appeared to be rather rough characters and I was hesitant to accept their offer, but the pressure to reach my goal outweighed my caution. As soon as we started moving, one of the men drew a revolver and showed it to me. "See this?" he said. "Any funny business from you, and I'll use it." If his intent was to intimidate me, he was wasting his time. But I was mystified. What funny business did he mean? Seeing my puzzled expression, he explained that a lot of women on the road were taking advantage of their benefactors by threatening to claim that they had been transported across state lines against their will, in violation of the Mann Act. Of course, a proper "settlement" would preclude such claims. Today, the threat of suing for sexual harassment has supplanted the Mann Act.

After being reassured that "funny business" was not on my agenda, we conversed like old friends, but not for long. Their destination took them north while I continued west.

Dusk was falling when a modest sedan pulled to a stop beside me. Two youngish men in the front seat asked if I was going far. "California," I replied. Well, they could take me as far as Salt Lake City, about six hundred miles. I had the back seat to myself and could sleep off and on. The men took turns driving and I got the impression that they were returning to duty on a government project in New Mexico.

In Salt Lake City, I spent my last quarter for a cup of coffee and a newspaper, and cleaned up in a public restroom. With luck, I'd be in California by nightfall.

On the outskirts of the city with cars zooming by, I began to wonder if my luck hadn't run out. I didn't have to wonder long. The people in Utah may be friendly, but they have the unfriendliest gnats in creation. Great swarms of the little "beasties" assaulted me, took a bite, retreated, and came back for "seconds." About the time that I had resigned myself to becoming a sun-bleached carcass on the salt flats of Utah, a middle-aged couple in a sedan rescued me from those miserable gnats.

When we reached the Nevada state line, they stopped and let me walk across the line, then picked me up on the other side. The Mann Act cast a long shadow in those days.

At Wells, they turned south off the Lincoln Highway, and I trudged westward. At least, there were no gnats. Eventually, an old rattle-trap truck overtook me. The driver was a fat, middle-aged man of Mexican or Portuguese extraction. Again, I was reluctant to accept the lift, but decided to take a calculated risk. As soon as we were on our way, he told me that he was a rancher and he needed a cook. From his point of view, cooking for him was much more desirable than continuing on my way to California. From my point of view, it did not compute at all. Realizing that he probably had no intention of stopping to let me out before we reached his ranch, I began watching the road behind us for approaching traffic. I had decided to bail out of the slow-moving vehicle as soon as a car appeared in the rear view mirror. I would be thrown forward by the fall, the rancher would brake, and the other motorist would stop to see if we needed help. As it turned out, this scenario was unnecessary. Suddenly, like a mirage, a gas station appeared on the horizon. I told the rancher that I needed to use the facilities. While he waited for me, I told the attendant that I did not want to continue with the man in the truck. The attendant relayed my message to the driver and he left. Since I was not sure that the man might not just drive out of sight and wait for me to come walking by again, I asked the attendant for permission to rest there a while. He welcomed a chance to talk, and I have always been a good listener.

When I deemed it safe, I continued on my way. I walked several miles before an open touring car came by. It contained three men, definitely under the influence. They were headed for Reno to continue partying. Hoping that my luck would hold, I got in the back seat. The only time that the driver hit the road was when he crossed it, but he didn't speed and the traffic was scarce. Suffice it to say that I heaved a giant sigh of relief as they delivered me to a street corner in Reno.

As I stood there trying to get my bearings, I heard someone call my name.

"Maxine! What are you doing here?" It was Jessie Hansen, one of my former high school classmates. She knew where some of my foster relatives lived in Reno, and led the way. The Parrys made me welcome, fed me, and found some replacements for my worn-out sandals. I rested there three days before heading north to Alturas and Cedarville. A United Parcel Service truck picked me up outside the city limits and carried me to the Susanville "Y." Since he was loaded with baby chicks, all chirping simultaneously, the noise was deafening. I was not unhappy to change "horses" in mid-stream as it were. A Coca-Cola truck driver delivered me to Alturas. On the way to Cedarville, Fay Kennedy, daughter of Dr. Kennedy, gave me a ride. She whipped her father's Buick over Cedar Pass in record time, hitting eighty miles an hour between curves.

My first job was for Claude Mulkey, whose wife was in the hospital. He had a small dairy of seventeen cows and sold butterfat. One of Dad's first jobs in Surprise Valley was milking forty-four cows manually twice a day, but seventeen was enough for me. The cream separator was manually operated also and had to be washed and sterilized after each use. From washing the cows' udders before milking, to cleaning the barn, sanitizing the equipment, hygiene is top priority in the dairy business.

After that I took a temporary job at Leonard's Baths, a seasonal operation in spite of the pool being fed by mineral hot springs. Washing towels and rental swim suits, cleaning the cabanas, and keeping a weather eye on swimmers kept me busy. Although I could swim, I certainly wasn't qualified as a life guard. Fortunately only one occasion arose when such skills were needed. A party of three women arrived for an evening dip. I smelled alcohol on their breath but could not quantify their level of intoxication by smell alone. Not long after they entered the pool, one of them decided to drown herself. Her friends and I struggled to keep her afloat while she fought off our attempts to rescue her. A life guard could have smacked her in the jaw, but we were obliged to rely on perseverance to tire her out. Eventually, we dragged her out of the water, physically exhausted but still verbally abusive because we had saved her life.

In July, Roy Godfrey, Dorris Fulcher, and another miner from the North Star mining company came into George's Club looking for a cook. Mrs. Smith was quitting. George told them that I was between jobs, so I gathered up my belongings and went with them to Fort Bidwell and up High Grade Canyon to the Big Four mine, where we turned off to climb another mile and a half to the North Star mine, owned and operated by the Morrells of Los Angeles. They had constructed a large bunkhouse and office building separate from the mess hall, kitchen, and larder. Adjacent to the mine shaft itself was the engine room for the hoist. We had to park below the buildings because of the steep gradient and walk up to the mess hall. As Roy opened the door to the kitchen, a little old gray-haired lady suddenly threw up her hands to an image on the wall and cried out, "Oh, Mighty I Am, how many are there for dinner today?" I didn't know whether to laugh or run, so I froze. I did not hear any response to her question, but apparently she did. She turned to us for introductions and seemed a bit dismayed at my youth, but was so anxious to get shut of the place that she gave me her cook book to assuage her misgivings and left.

Usually there were fourteen present, seventeen when the bosses and bookkeeper came up from Los Angeles. I prepared three meals plus lunches for the swing shift, a twenty-hour day. My pay was eighty dollars a month and found.

One of the complaints that the miners had about Mrs. Smith was that she served little or no meat, as dictated by her religion, The Mighty I Am.

Like most men performing hard physical labor, they liked their meat. Gradually, I learned to cook with the help of the cook book and also from Roy's batching experience. He was the one who taught me to stir gravy with a fork and how to make sour dough bread. Although I later became known as the "Sour Dough Queen," my specialty was pies. Gene Staples, mining engineer from Grass Valley, was partial to lemon meringue pies, in round pieces, so when lemon pies were on the menu, I baked an extra pie for Gene. In trying to please everyone's palate, however, I nearly starved poor Harold "Happy" Miles. Everyone else liked garlic, but he didn't, and he was too courteous to complain. Poor man. Naturally I changed my cooking practices when I learned of his aversion, but I still feel guilty.

Little did I realize when I attended the Page murder trial that ten years later I would be cooking for one of the jurors, William "Bill" Crow. While most of the miners were local, mostly middle-aged men, there were two young "outsiders," Jack and Strom. If Strom ever spoke, I never heard him, but Jack made up for his friend's reticence. Soon he had antagonized everyone on the premises, including the cook. The situation reached crisis proportions when Gene threatened to quit. The rest of the men opted to hold a Kangaroo Court and "try" Jack *in absentia*.

Before Jack had been hired, the men had made friends with the wild chipmunks, buying peanuts for them when they got paid. The chipmunks had lost their fear of people, so when Jack held out his hand to one, it expected a peanut, not a live cigarette against its nose. This cruelty was only one in a long list of charges. One miner objected to Jack's using the public swimming pool because he had a venereal disease. Roy objected to him "hanging around the cook." By the time the opinion poll reached "Happy," he summed it up succinctly. "I just don't like the son-of-a-bitch." The verdict was unanimous. When the bosses arrived, they were met by a delegation of miners with an ultimatum: "Jack goes or everyone else does."

While no complaints had been lodged against Strom, he left with Jack anyway.

When Fair time in Cedarville rolled around, Roy provided transportation for the cook and other crew members without wheels. At the fair, he offered to let me use his car, a Nash-Lafayette sedan, to take Packy for a drive, and I was foolish enough to accept. We decided to go out to Vya. As I stepped on the brake to slow for a curve, the wheel locked, swerving the vehicle toward the bank. I over-corrected and the car rolled over on its side like a tired elephant. Except for banging my elbow against the door latch, no one was hurt. My next thought was, "Oh, my God! Barney's car."

While we discussed what to do, a car came along headed for Cedarville. It was decided that she should go back to town, while I walked to Vya, about a mile and a half, to see if someone could help get the car back on its wheels. The caretaker at Vya drove me to the Swinford Springs CC Camp, where I was invited to dine. I had no interest in food, but I could hardly expect the whole camp to forego their meal because of my problem. The only thing on the menu that I remember was celery sticks stuffed with peanut butter. After a year or two, the meal ended and men and material were mobilized to resolve my immediate problem. They drove to the accident site, tipped the car back on its wheels, and towed it to town to a garage. The main damage was a "sprung frame," which was never corrected but cost $200 anyway. No one in those days carried auto insurance, so I now owed $200 and the mine was closing for the winter. I tried frantically to find another job or to borrow the money to clear my obligation to Roy. No luck. So I accepted his proposal of marriage.

CHAPTER 11

"For the intent and purpose of the law
Hath full relation to the penalty,
Which here appeareth due upon the bond."

> *The Merchant of Venice*, Act IV, Scene I.
> William Shakespeare

Roy and I were married September 4, 1937, in Lakeview, Oregon. He was twenty years older than I, thirty-seven to my seventeen, but I tried to make the best of a bad situation at first. However, when I tried to talk to him, he would say, "If you're talking to me, you'll have to speak English." Then he would laugh at his own wit. Needless to say, I got the message. Apparently he believed that women, like children, should be seen and not heard.

Roy was hired as caretaker at the mine. By October 1, we were snowed in, except on snow-shoes. The gradient of the slopes was so steep that skiers had to herringbone up the mountain side. The snow continued, to a depth of nine feet at the mine. Like moles, we had to tunnel our way to the surface.

In due course, I became pregnant and had "morning sickness" for the next six months. The baby was due June 26, and we were snow-bound until June 13. Fortunately the baby was ten days late.

We moved to an apartment in the Fort Bidwell Hotel managed by John Reynolds. The mine had closed and Roy found a job at a sawmill south of Canby, California.

My son arrived July 6, 1938, a natural easy delivery at home with Dr. Kennedy and Esther Burgoyne, nurse, in attendance. When I complained about the ten-day confinement period, Dr. Kennedy told me, "Enjoy it while you can. It's the only rest a mother ever gets."

As soon as the new heir was ready to travel, we moved to the logging camp, where we lived in bunkhouses built of cull lumber, now called "knotty pine."

Soon I was pregnant again, in spite of Roy's efforts at birth control (*coitus interruptus*). But no morning sickness this time around. I had discovered O.M. tablets, an herbal laxative that solved my irregularity problems permanently.

When the mill closed down for the winter, we moved back to Fort Bidwell. On January 18, 1939, Miss Abbie Godfrey died at the general hospital at the age of eighty-six.[84] She was Roy's paternal aunt, an educated woman and accomplished poet.

On July 1, 1939, my second son was born, same building, different apartment, with Dr. Kennedy and Esther Burgoyne again officiating. But this time there were complications. The umbilical cord was coiled around the baby's neck. Recently I heard a doctor expounding on television that without modern technology, babies in such situations were doomed. For his information, a good doctor is better than technology any day.

Since birth is a natural process, I was not "drugged up" and could cooperate with the doctor. He explained the situation. The baby's head was "born" but the cord, wrapped around the neck, was too short to permit further progress. Therefore, the cord had to be cut and delivery completed instantaneously, so that the baby's lungs could start replacing the oxygen normally delivered through the cord. Timing was everything, to prevent brain damage from loss of oxygen to the brain. When the next contraction came, I bore down as hard as I could. The doctor clamped, cut, and pulled. The baby was delivered, slightly blue. Kennedy held him up by the heels and spanked him, unnecessarily. Steve was already yelling lustily. The doctors instruction "to keep him crying" was also redundant. Soon the blue was gone and Steve was a healthy blood-red color. He suffered no ill effects, then or later.

After Steve was born, Roy terminated our conjugal relationship completely by moving into a separate bedroom. Abstinence was and is a fool-proof method of birth control. This situation continued until we divorced some eight years later.

In the meantime, we moved into a house a block or two south. Roy's work kept him away from home except on weekends. On one such visit, I was in the kitchen preparing a meal. Charles, my oldest son, was just learning to walk, and just tall enough to reach things on the edge of the table. I had carelessly left an open box of rice within his reach and he knocked the package over on the floor, spilling the contents. Roy grabbed him by the arm and threw him through the doorway into the living room. Fortunately, he landed on Roy's bedroll and was uninjured. But I went into orbit. I jumped on Roy's back and threatened to kill him if he ever did that again. No animal was ever more primitive in defense of its young than I.

Roy never touched the boys again in anger, but he vented his spleen in other ways. Once he stamped a new window blind to smithereens because it wouldn't roll properly. Another time he tried to punish our dog, an Australian Shepherd-Collie mix, for barking. Instead of taking the abuse in dog-like fashion, he fought back. If I had not intervened, one of them would have died there.

Later I told Roy's father, Charley Godfrey, Sr., former clerk in Dennehy's Store in Cedarville until he retired to Fort Bidwell, about the episode with the dog. The old man shook his head sadly. "Don't know where Roy gets that temper. Must get it from me, though. The Old Lady still has all of hers." Truth is often spoken in jest.

Nor was bad temper all that she imparted to her offspring. Two of her five children were also epileptic: Nellie, who married Martin Anderson, and Charley, Jr., who was single and still lived at home. Since Charley was a frequent visitor at our house, it was no surprise that he would have a seizure while there. The first indication that I had that anything was wrong was a sharp, pungent odor like ozone, after a lightning strike, followed by grand mal. About all I knew to do was to keep something, preferably leather, between his teeth so that he wouldn't bite his tongue, and to try to keep him off the stove. He was strong as an ox and I was exhausted by the time the seizure ended and he lapsed into unconsciousness. Naturally, he was unable to go home in this condition so I made up a bed for him in the living room. These seizures continued at intervals all night and he slept all day, while I chopped wood, pumped water, washed baby clothes (both boys were still in Birdseye diapers), cooked, cleaned, and ironed. At night the seizures started again, becoming more violent and longer in duration. Finally I sought help from the neighbors. Every night for nearly three months, two of the neighbors spent the nights in a seemingly endless struggle to protect him from injury. We had no medication and I wasn't sure that restraints like straight jackets were safe, so we endured. Eventually, someone blew the whistle and Roy transported Charley to Portland, Oregon, where his sister, Mertie, and her husband lived. I assume that Charley was hospitalized.

Anyway the seizures stopped. His ordeal cost him about fifty pounds and I lost thirty. Besides the weight loss, I developed a sharp pain in my back. I couldn't eat or sleep for the pain. I went to three different doctors (Dr. Kennedy was not available), and they all looked down my throat and discovered that I had enlarged tonsils and prescribed a tonsillectomy. Since I was enlarged all over and never had tonsil problems, I sought a fourth opinion. Miracle of miracles. Dr. Phil McKenny looked at my back! Due to a fall on the ice when I was twelve (I had been paralyzed for three days), my lower back was a mass of scar tissue, damaged vertebrae, and dislocated hip bone. The doctor said that it was a miracle that I could walk at all. The strain of dealing with Charley's seizures had locked in a muscle spasm, like a permanent charley horse in my back. The doctor gave me a shot of curare to relax the cramp and told me not to lift or to climb stairs. By being careful, I avoided a recurrence of the problem and I still have my tonsils!

That fall, Dr. Kennedy's grandson, Larry Linville, was born to his daughter, Fay, and her husband, Harry, at Ojai, California.[85] Little did we expect that infant Larry would become the "fraternizing, whining, Major Burns in the movie and long-running TV series of M*A*S*H."[86]

The following summer we moved to the Leonard Creek district south of Denio, Nevada, where George Matheson and Tom Jones operated a gold mine. The location of the mine was inaccurately reported in the *Alturas Plaindealer* as the "Trinity Claims on High Grade, formerly known as the Big 4"[87] in California. Except for the geographical error, the rest of the story was accurate. Matheson and Associates of Fort Bidwell sank a 500' shaft, installed a cyanide plant, and shipped an ingot of gold, valued at $512.00 to the mint in San Francisco November 7, 1940.[88]

We spent the winter there until we were notified that Roy's father had passed away March 20, 1941, and we returned to Fort Bidwell to attend his funeral. After the funeral, we moved into the large two-story house across the street from Lowell's Store and next door to Roy and Violet Baty.

Before hunting season started that fall, I received a letter from my Uncle Max Heald saying that he and a friend would be deer hunting in the area and would stop by for a visit. They arrived one evening. As Uncle Max admitted later, he did not believe that my mother and his mother had kept my existence a secret, but my strong resemblance to his baby sister convinced him. He told me that she had died June 8, 1941, in San Francisco of chronic bilateral pulmonary tuberculosis at the age of thirty-nine.

Following the Japanese attack on Pearl Harbor, December 7, 1941, Uncle Max joined the Sea Bees there. He sent me some money for Christmas, which I used to buy a round-trip ticket to Oakland and Richmond to visit family over the holidays.

During World War II, Greyhound provided bus service between Alturas and Redding. Going down Burney Mountain we met a log truck which forced our vehicle into the bank to avoid a collision, jamming the door shut. Since I was seated directly behind the driver, I appreciated his evasive action.

Besides my Uncle Wilbert and his family at Oakland, George and Wally Wood were both employed in the shipyards near Richmond.

When my boys and I arrived on New Year's Day, Uncle Wilbert gave me a red carpet welcome. Then our conversation turned to his earlier visit to Cedarville when I lived with the Harrises and Grandfather had left an historic newspaper in my care. Uncle Wilbert seemed to think that I still had it. I assured him that the document had been returned as instructed. Once he was convinced that I no longer had it, my welcome ended. I called George to come and get me. At that time he and his new wife, Bernice, also had two boys, Dale and Bobby. While there, Wally took me to visit "Frosty" Poore, Marine, who was an early casualty in the Pacific Theater of Operations. Frosty was a senior when I was a "freshie" in Surprise Valley High and a local hero. Although he had lost an eye, he was his usual charming self, trying to put me at ease, while I stood there tongue-tied. Hearing about the war was one thing. Seeing the endless corridors dividing the rows of wounded men in Quonset style buildings was devastating.

However, it was soon time for me to head home to Fort Bidwell. By the time we reached Redding on our return trip, I had a raging fever, fell asleep in the bus station, and missed the bus. Somewhat rested by my nap but still broke, I started walking with the boys in tow. Soon a Highway Patrol Officer stopped and picked us up and took us as far as Fall River. After that a rancher in a truck offered us a lift in the back of his truck. It's cold in the mountains in January, so I took off my coat to bundle up the boys. They survived the trip with no ill effects, but I had double pneumonia. I spent the next thirty days flat on my back. Roy applied mustard poultices and "sweat" me, while I drifted in a red haze. Needless to say I recovered.

In September we moved to a logging camp on the west side of Goose Lake where the logs were floated across the lake to the mill at Willow Ranch. My friend, Ruby Green, and her family were already living there.

Her husband, Ernest was mechanic, candy-wagon driver, and trouble shooter. So when her washing machine, better known as the "divorce machine," went on the blink, Ernie tried to repair it. He hauled it to the shop and gave the motor a complete overhaul. He brought it back, the engine running like a top. Ruby filled the tub with water and clothes and turned it on. Nothing happened. Then it was taken to a local repair shop in Lakeview, and eventually to its source in Klamath Falls (not a Maytag, obviously). They "fixed" it and returned it. Except it still wouldn't work. Ruby was fit to be tied, or should I be politically correct and say "stressed?" Whatever.

"Please just look at it," she begged. While I wore many hats, from Dr. Godfrey to barber to pie-woman extraordinaire, a mechanic's chapeau was not one of them. However, I agreed "to look." I looked at the loaded machine, pushed the switch to "On." Nothing. Since the engine was doing its thing, that left the switch or the gyrator. I didn't have the tools with which to attack the switch so I zeroed in on the dasher. I told Ruby to empty the tub of clothes and water. Then I pulled the gyrator off the spindle and examined it visually and tactilely. No sharp edges, which indicated wear on the tongues and grooves of the inter-facing parts. I found a discarded Prince Albert tobacco tin, cut out a strip, moulded it around the spindle, and forced the gyrator back on. We reloaded the wash and pushed the lever. Worked like a charm! Not because I was smarter, but because I started where the problem was. Sometimes the simplest solution is the right one.

When Ernie came home that evening, Ruby showed him what I had done. Grudgingly he admitted, "Not bad, for a woman."

Where did the washer get the soubriquet "divorce machine?" Well, Herb and Marcella Wood bought it, separated, and sold it to George and Dorris Wood who later separated and sold it to Ernest and Ruby Green. The third time proved the charm. The machine had found a happy home at last.

In October, I made a break for freedom, taking the boys with me and leaving a note for Roy telling him where to find the pick-up in Alturas. I got a job as waitress at the Post Office Cafe, operated by Jimmie Brown, the only diner authorized by the Government to stay open around the clock to accommodate the railroad men who had top priority for service. This was war time and transport of war materials was vital to national security. I worked the graveyard shift at 35 cents an hour. Without the tips, no one could have survived. By day, I took in ironing, work that I could do at home while caring for the kids. I discovered that I could manage on four hours sleep a day and work twenty. I read the boys to sleep (they preferred

Homer's *Iliad*) before a neighbor took over, and I returned home as they were waking up. Roy spent his weekends trying to effect a reconciliation with threats and false accusations. When that failed he sued for divorce and custody of the boys. My attorney filed demurrers.

Sometime during this separation Roy had an accident with a chain saw and lost three fingers of his right hand. He got a settlement which gave him a financial advantage in our civil suit, which dragged on and on.

Then out of the blue, I received a letter from my long lost brother, Gene. He was in boot camp in Camp McCain, Mississippi. He explained that grandmother had died the previous year and when going through her effects, the family had found the letters that I had written to her in the bottom of a trunk. Although Gene was almost two years older than I, he didn't remember having a baby sister. Naturally the Nevada address was no help in locating my current whereabouts. Sixteen years had elapsed and I had changed my name, but he finally located me about the time he was inducted into the Army. Later he was stationed in Germany. We corresponded faithfully until he was mustered out November 5, 1945. Then he sent me a telegram for bus fare from San Francisco to Fort Bidwell, pending receipt of his mustering out pay. Unfortunately, the Western Union office was located in Kober's store, which was closed that afternoon for a funeral! I didn't receive his wire until the following day. Apparently, Gene assumed that I ignored his message, and he dropped out of my life again.

However, I am getting ahead of myself. In the spring of 1943, night crews from the box factory carried the rumor that the local airstrip was being extended to accommodate military jets carrying special cargo, all top secret, of course. Speculation ran rampant about the nature of the special cargo, but I doubt that anyone expected the Brooklyn Dodgers in full uniform and converging on the Niles Hotel. According to the grapevine, they had hitched a ride on a military jet to the west coast on an exhibition tour for the war effort. There was no fanfare, because officially they weren't there.

In late June, my oldest son, age four, developed appendicitis. I took him to the doctor who said the leucocyte count did not support my tactile diagnosis, which I had been taught by Dr. Kennedy. Two days later, the appendix ruptured. Even though it was an emergency, it was another fourteen hours before my son reached the operating room. Peritonitis was only one of the resulting complications. Charles refused to eat, and when I visited him he would ask if I was taking him home. When I explained that the doctor wouldn't let me, he turned his face to the wall and said no more. After twenty-three more days of physical deterioration, I told the doctor that I was taking my son home. He asked me to sign a waiver of responsibility and I did. This time when Charles asked me if I was taking him home, I gathered him up in my arms and walked out. As soon as we got home, he started eating and within twenty-four hours he was sitting up and playing with his brother.

In the meantime, my attorney had run out of demurrers and Roy had persuaded the judge that if he were awarded custody of the boys I would return to him. Since courts are allegedly supposed to effect reconciliations whenever possible, the judge ruled in his favor. With Charles still convalescing, I had no choice but to return.

We moved to the E. G. Scammon ranch at Cowhead Lake where Mr. Scammon raised purebred Hereford bulls for sale. The young animals had to be trained to "show," a job which naturally fell to me because I had a "way" with livestock, except horses. Horses are prone to hysteria under stress such as fire or electrical storms, and "shying" or "bolting" for no reason. I relate better to rationality in animals as well as people.

Earlier that year, Mrs. M. J. Decious, Fort Bidwell Postmaster for thirty-seven years, resigned so I took the Civil Service examination for the position. I was interviewed at the Scammon ranch by a federal agent, who looked like the All-American stereotype of a Mafia boss. However, he had credentials and tough questions. "Why did I want the job?" The answer was for financial independence but I thought that the truth might imply marital instability which would jeopardize my chances of appointment. "Peace of mind?" was the best alternative I could muster. The poor man probably thought that a "piece" of mind was all that I had. Anyway, time dragged by and John Mankin was appointed Acting Postmaster. By the time I received the appointment, I had changed my mind about spending the rest of my life in Fort Bidwell.

Naturally, Mankin saw the official notice before I did and recognized its significance.

The following night there was a dance at the local hall. Everyone attended, even Mankin who didn't dance because of a disability. As I danced by where he was sitting, I stopped and told him that the job was his if he wanted it. I didn't. At least I made one man happy in my lifetime. He was so grateful that I was embarrassed.

From Scammon's ranch, we moved to Harry Schadler's adjoining ranch, and then to Fort Bidwell where Roy bought the Harry Larimore property, a two-story frame house situated on a couple acres of land with riparian rights to Bidwell Creek at the foot of school house hill. Since Charles began school that fall, the location was serendipitous. If memory serves, Mrs. Whaley was his first teacher.

CHAPTER 12

". . . O, it is excellent
To have a giant's strength; but it is tyrannous
To use it like a giant."

> *Measure for Measure*, Act II, Scene II.
> William Shakespeare

Although I had learned to drive when I was eight years old and had driven intermittently ever since, I had never had an operator's license. On May 24, 1944, I decided to legalize my driving status. I had my new glasses so that I could pass the vision test, and I had no qualms about the written part of the examination, but I was dreading the driving test.

Since the Department of Motor Vehicles was located in Alturas, I did not arrive there until the afternoon. I sailed through the vision and written tests and was waiting for an officer to monitor my driving skills, when the radio started squawking. I couldn't understand a word it said, but the three or four Highway Patrol Officers present did. The one who was processing my application said, "Can you drive?" I responded affirmatively and he signed the form approving my license. Then they all burned rubber north to the Tulelake segregation center where a Japanese internee, Shiochi James Okomoto, 30, was fatally shot by a United States Army sentry in the line of duty.[89]

As former internee, Masuda, recently recalled, the Japanese Americans lived in "flimsy barracks of tar paper and pine . . . no privacy . . . and when the wind blew, the sand would crawl up through the floor, the doors and the windows like ants."[90] A ten-foot high chain-link fence enclosed the segregation center with guard towers at appropriate intervals.

After the War, the Government authorized the salvage of internee housing by local farmers and ranchers. Kesner and Maxine Toney and I decided to take advantage of the offer, figuring that the scrap lumber for fuel would justify the 130-mile trip from Fort Bidwell. It didn't. Originally constructed of thin beaverboard tacked to thin slats, it was no match for the Tulelake weather, wind-blown dust in summer and snow in winter.

In 1928, when we took our trip to Montana, Tulelake was exactly that, a shallow lake with reeds and tules providing a natural habitat for migratory water fowl and earlier a source of food and fiber for the Modoc Indians. The road was a one-lane graveled trail hugging one side of the basin. But the government reclamation process had already begun. By degrees, the basin was drained and plowed up for field crops, and a wall of blowing dust replaced the rippling lake surface of yesterday. In recent years, overhead sprinklers have supplanted surface irrigation with a commensurate reduction in wind erosion of the basin. Now crop dusters with herbicides, insecticides, and pesticides contribute to the local ecolocide.

Not long after we moved to town, I accidentally chopped my right foot while splitting wood, severing the artery and tendon to my big toe. The blood frothed forth in vivid florescent orange, capped by billowing clouds of white foam. For a few seconds, I stood transfixed by the sheer beauty of the living geyser; then I dropped the axe and applied manual pressure to both sides of the slice. The boys were playing nearby so I told them to go get Mrs. Sweeney, our nearest neighbor and close friend. The boys started to stall as kids will when interrupted at play, and then they saw the blood. I'm sure they set a record on their way but I didn't have a stop watch. Maggie did not waste any time getting there, either. While I maintained pressure on the wound she removed my shoe and sock and bandaged my foot with clean tea towels. The next morning my foot was swollen as large as a dish pan and black with congested blood. I finally managed to ease a large buckled overshoe on my foot so that I could do chores. I had two cows to milk and bummer lambs to feed beside the usual household duties. My foot was tender to walk on for a few days, but it healed perfectly with minimal scarring.

More serious was my second son's experience with a dynamite cap. It was Sunday, May 18, and I was working in the garden. The boys came to me with a round tin container resembling a chewing tobacco can. When I removed the lid, I saw a full can of percussion caps. Aware of the danger, but at a loss on how to dispose of them before Roy came home, I warned the boys not to touch them again or they "could be blown to Kingdom Come." A short time later, I heard an explosion in front of the house. I rushed to the scene. Steve had lit a match to a cap and lost some fingers and flesh from his left hand. The explosion had ruptured blood vessels in his eyes and shrapnel pitted his face and chest. Fortunately he was wearing bibbed overalls and a suede leather jacket or the chest injuries would have been worse.

As I wrapped his damaged hand in a towel, a neighbor volunteered to call Walt Lowell, who had flown for General Eisenhower in England, to fly us to Alturas but I declined. I was afraid that the high altitude would increase the risk of hemorrhaging. While I loaded the boys into the pick-up, the neighbor said he would call Dean Wylie, druggist in Cedarville, to provide first aid. In Cedarville, Dean replaced the bandage and alerted the hospital in Alturas that I was on my way. Luckily there was no traffic on Cedar Pass because I "straightened" out the curves as I drove.

Dr. Phil McKenny, surgeon, was home from his service in the Pacific and did a magnificent job of salvaging and restoring the mutilated hand. Although parts of most of the fingers were missing, it was never a handicap. He even learned to type. For the bean-counters, the total hospital and doctor bill was $26.00.

That fall Ernest Server, better known as "Buck" Daggert, Deputy Sheriff for ten years, succeeded L. G. McDowell as Modoc County probation and truant officer.[91], "Buck" wore many hats during his career as peace officer, but he never wore a gun. He still managed to apprehend some of the most wanted thugs of the thirties. In 1928, he was a local contender from Ballard's Mill to fight Jack Harmon of Lakeview. Daggert weighed in at 185 pounds and measured six feet, three inches.[92] At one time, he was sparring partner for Maxie Baer, heavy weight boxing champion. In 1932, Buck and his wife, the former Maude Hawkins, was employed on the Essex ranch.[93] At the Lakeview Roundup that fall, he won first prize in the bronc-riding contest.[94]

Another tradition in Modoc County and long-time friend was Jimmie Washoe, *de facto* chief of the Paiute tribe. Born at the turn of the century, I doubt that he ever missed a rodeo or a round-up. His father was a Chinese laundryman and his mother Paiute. Dad and Mother had known Jimmie most of his life and he was welcomed like "one of the family." Jockey-sized, he was never far from a horse. He was hospitalized at least once by a horse and once by a gunshot through the stomach at Fort Bidwell.[95] Jimmie will long be remembered for his wit and humor.

One of the most decorated soldiers of World War II was Blazer Paddy, native of Fort Bidwell. He was one of a handful of survivors of a troop ship, sunk by the Japanese, who had managed to swim under the burning oil surrounding the sinking vessel. When he returned, the town gave a reception in his honor. Later when I was cooking for Peterson's hay crew, Blazer was one of the crew. He declared that I was the best pie cook in the world. Naturally I was flattered, but I didn't think that my "war" pies were up to their usual standard of excellence. Having to substitute honey for sugar in all recipes had been a real challenge. Honey in meringue gave it a faint green cast, and the smell of hot honey still turns *me* slightly green.

Unfortunately, alcohol succeeded where the war failed. Blazer died an alcoholic.

In Cedarville, Dr. Walter J. Hamilton took over Dr. Kennedy's former practice. Fresh out of med school, he was somewhat pompous. So when I took my boys to his office and asked for a prescription for pinworms, he gave me a lecture on parasitic worms and informed me that only a doctor could identify the specific cause of the helminthiasis. He went through the ritual of scotch tape sampling and microscopic examination, and then burst out in frustration, "How could you know they were pinworms?" Explaining that I could see them without a microscope, that I was interested in all knowledge, including medicine, and that Dr. Kennedy had taught me many tricks of the trade, such as the tactile test for appendicitis, would not have salved his wounded ego, so I kept quiet. Without further ado, he wrote out a prescription and started preparing his black bag for an unscheduled trip to the Fort Bidwell elementary school where a wide infestation of *oxyuris vermicularis* awaited him.

When I was attending high school in Cedarville, I frequently stopped by Dr. Kennedy's office on my way home. If he wasn't busy with a patient, he would answer my questions. At that time, I was considering becoming a neuro-surgeon. Dr. Kennedy believed that women were not physically or emotionally equipped to handle the rigors of the medical profession. When he was serving in the trenches in France during World War I, women in labor came to him to be delivered. Newborn babies mingled with the dead and dying in the mud and blood of the trenches. He recommended a career in nursing instead, but the bed-pan routine did not appeal to me. Then, like Socrates, he asked the key question. "If you needed neuro-surgery and two equally-qualified doctors, a woman and a man, were available, which would you choose?" I didn't answer. It wasn't necessary. Maybe a career in journalism would be a challenging alternative?

Of course, marriage had put my educational aspirations on hold, but I could still read. Besides reading everything in the local library, I joined a Classics Book Club and took a home correspondence course in Journalism. The latter was a waste of time and money, like most self-improvement programs, but that in itself was a learning experience.

Unlike most females, I never had the patience to fiddle with my hair, so Dorris took me to a barber when I was twelve to get what was called a "boyish bob." This hair style required little attention and kept the hair out of my face and off my neck. However, it did entail regular trips to the barber shop. After Roy and I were married, he cut my hair and I cut his. Soon other men were coming for haircuts, usually when Roy was home, so that people wouldn't gossip. Otherwise, they had to drive to Cedarville and pay a dollar for a haircut. I didn't charge for the service, but the men usually left a fifty cent tip. In conjunction with other odd jobs, I managed to earn some pin money since Roy provided only food and lodging. He maintained charge accounts at Lowell's Mercantile and Kober's Dry Goods. However, I still had to ask his permission before I could charge a pair of shoes. Since he kept his income a secret, only he knew what we could afford. Our luxuries were a radio to keep abreast of the news and a subscription to *Liberty* magazine.

World War II finally ended and thanks to the SNAFU with Western Union, my hopes of a reunion with my long-lost brother also ended.

In 1946, my friend, Erma McTimmonds, now married to Charles "Chuck" Hickerson, and Assistant Postmaster of the Alturas Post Office, was elected President of the American Legion Auxiliary.[96]

CHAPTER 13

"Not he that sets his foot upon her back.
The smallest worm will turn, being trodden on."

King Henry VI (Part 3), Act II, Scene II.
William Shakespeare

On June 20, 1947, I crossed my Rubicon. Even slaves and criminals won their freedom after ten years of indenture, so I walked out with my purse and the clothes on my back. Roy refused to let me take even personal pictures or papers.

Within a mile or so, a salesman en route to Alturas picked me up. Naturally he was curious, so I briefly explained my situation, which he summed up succinctly: Sex without love is service without satisfaction.

When we arrived in Alturas, he dropped me off at the Unemployment Office where Jim Payne, head of the Department, drove me the ten miles to the Sam Merlini ranch where a cook was needed. Jim prided himself on instant placement.

Within a few days, Roy brought the boys to the ranch and left them. Not long after that, Bill Edwards also went to work there. Having the proverbial gift of gab, he soon captivated the boys with his war stories and anecdotes. At eight and nine, they were looking for a "hero," a male role model. Here was one who had "been there, done that," and was willing to spend his free time talking about his experiences. And his stories were true. As Technician 5th Grade in the 441st Anti-Aircraft Artillery Armored Weapon Battalion; he had served from Africa to the Rhineland hitting all the hot spots between: Rome, Arno, Sicily, Naples, Foggia, Southern France, and Central Europe. His decorations included the Croix de Guerre, Fourragere, Distinguished Unit Badge, European, African, and Middle Eastern Campaign Medal with one Arrowhead and the Good Conduct Medal. After his enlistment in 1942, he was offered Officers' training, but he declined on the basis that he didn't want the responsibility of command. However, he did take Commando training.

Nor was he the only "hero" in the Edwards family. All of his brothers served in one branch or another. While his brother, Ken, served only two months in the National Guard before being discharged for poor vision, Rich, who had lost an eye in a childhood accident, was drafted into the 1961st Service Command as a Marksman guarding prisoners in the Non-Combatant Unit in San Diego. Roger was in the Navy during the War and later joined the Army. Under age, Allan volunteered for Special Services for Shock Troop training with the 101st Airborne Division, 506 Parachute Regiment. He was in the hospital in England following a training jump injury when his CO decided to make a "drop" behind enemy lines in France. Allan was rousted from the sick bay, given an obsolete gun, jump knife, and a chocolate D-Bar, and his marching orders. The Paratroopers landed behind Utah Beach which the Germans had flooded for a tank trap. In the resulting machine gun fire and exploding mines, Allan was taken prisoner on June 6, 1944, and held until August 1945, when the Russians "liberated" him. Today he is the proud father of the first millionaire in the Edwards family.

In contrast, Roy was a man of few words, except in anger, and had little time to spare being a father.

While I was well aware that men often try to use kids as stepping stones to their mother's affections, I do not attribute such guile to Bill. He just liked to talk, and soon I became part of the audience.

Dad had classified men into three groups: thinkers, doers, and talkers, and warned me against the latter. But after ten years in a verbal vacuum, I was susceptible to the Scheherazade factor as well.

When Bill proposed, I accepted, but first I had to get a divorce. Bill took the boys and me to Reno for the mandatory six-week residency requirement. As soon as Roy received the interlocutory decree, he came to Reno and took the boys. Nevada jurisdiction did not extend to child custody in out-of-state cases.

Shortly after I arrived in Reno to establish residency, I was notified that Dad had died August 24, 1947, in Yankton, South Dakota, of hypostatic pneumonia.

To pay attorney's fees and the rent, I worked at Washoe General Hospital and the Sunshine Laundry. When the decree was final, Bill and I crossed the street to a marriage chapel and were married. My landlady, Sally Shaddack, was one of the witnesses.

I wish I could say "and they lived happily ever after." Unfortunately, I already realized that I'd done it again; I'd made another mistake.

Since we had both been working when we met, I assumed that we would both find new jobs, save our money, and build a life. So much for WASPish assumptions.

As a Veteran, Bill was eligible for a short-term Government program which paid $20.00 a week for thirty weeks, or *vice versa*. He decided that with this "seed" money, we would go into the rabbit and chicken business up at Ballard's Reservoir. Formerly a booming sawmill site, only the old donkey engine, a few narrow gauge rails, and collapsing cabins were left to mark its demise. An earlier entrepreneur with equally unrealistic hallucinations, had built some kennels for a Boarding and Grooming facility for pets, mainly dogs. These kennels made excellent hutches for a dozen or so breeding stock of New Zealand white rabbits. The chicks could make do in boxes until we could patch up better accommodations. Our own housing was the only semi-intact bunk house still standing, a ten-by-twelve foot structure without doors or windows. The open windows provided fresh air and Bill nailed some planks together for a door, with either rubber or leather hinges. Our bed was a wooden frame filled with pine boughs, our stove an old gas tank with one end cut out and a stove pipe hole in the other end, our dishes mainly recycled tin cans, a decor straight out of Hobo Jungle 1A. We carried water from the reservoir, a somewhat unsanitary source. In similar situations, pioneers had dug a surface well some ten feet from the main body of water and waited for the filtered water to seep into the catchment basin which was then covered to prevent contamination from above. Being a highly skilled "catskinner," it did not occur to Bill to dig this well with a shovel which we had. No, only a D-8 Caterpillar would do, or maybe a D-6. While he cogitated on how to get a "cat," I dug the hole and devised the cover.

Being a "doer" myself, the idleness was driving me out of my skull, so I decided to build a brooder house for the chicks. The original headquarters of the mill had been built of premium quality lumber, knot-free tongue and groove flooring, full sized studs and boards. With basic hand tools, hammer, saw, level and square, I constructed a portable brooder house on skids so that it could be relocated. Since there was no electricity, a wood heater was centrally located with protective screen. The building had large windows on all four sides with storm shutters. Since few wood stoves held enough fuel to last overnight, I had to restoke the heater at least once a night. Other than this inconvenience, my first construction project was quite successful. When we moved away, the Dorrises, local ranchers, bought my brooder house and skidded it to their place with a tractor.

Less successful was the rabbit production, or should I say reproduction? Instead of a litter of ten or twelve young per doe per month as Bill had projected, a doe did well to produce a litter every two months, with six to eight fryers reaching the market. When winter made the roads impassable, we carried the dressed fryers out on foot to Canby, a trek of six to eight miles. Our income didn't even keep food on the table, let alone pay the feed bill at the Co-op. After months of eating pancakes and meat drippings, I complained so I feel partially responsible for what followed. Bill poached a deer and got caught. He was fined a hundred dollars, which we didn't have. He called Leo Donovan, a former employer in Tulelake, who loaned him the money. We sold our livestock and moved to Tulelake so that Bill could work off the loan.

While I missed the boys beyond words, I was thankful that they were not sharing our deprivation.

Our first abode was at Stronghold, site of the Modoc War in 1872-73, the only Indian war of consequence in California. For approximately six months, a rugged band of seventy-one Modoc Indians stood off an army of one thousand soldiers and volunteers.[97] On page 20 of the same publication, "fifty-three Modoc warriors" held off a thousand troops. Whatever the actual number of braves involved, the standing joke in the basin is a one-liner: "We fought the Indians for this and we lost. We got it."

Besides the blowing dust, residents had to cope with mineralized water which one had to hold one's nose to drink and turned every surface and fabric orange, except the human skin. In the last fifty years, potable water has been piped in and sprinkler systems have settled most of the dust.

Bill was not just a "catskinner." He was an artist with heavy equipment. Whether he was leveling a field or building a dam, his finesse would put a cake decorator to shame. And he didn't even need surveyors' stakes! In recognition of his expertise, Donovan paid him $2.00 an hour instead of the standard rate of $1.25, plus an extra hour for service, which many operators tended to neglect. Also, Donovan didn't "boss" him. Leo made a point of hiring men who knew what they were doing and then leaving them alone to do it.

Other employers were less understanding and less generous, and Bill was unemployed more often than not. His philosophy about low-paying jobs was that "if he was going on the bum, he might as well leave the work out of it." This independent attitude may be fine for a single man, but hardly a sound foundation for matrimony.

Later Leo contracted out his equipment to build the Carpenter reservoir near Canby. Besides his ranch east of Canyon Creek (now Cal-Pines), Leo owned property in Tulelake and a residence in Olean, Oregon.

When I became pregnant, Donovan offered Bill a salaried position as caretaker on the Canyon Creek spread.

Since childhood, I had planned my family: two boys and a red-headed girl, which I would spoil rotten! Well, I had the two boys and on August 10, 1949, I had my red-headed girl. Since the boys were born, laws had been passed that said that babies had to be born in hospitals. Being basically law-abiding, I went to the hospital in Alturas. Within minutes of her delivery, my daughter was laughing out loud to the astonishment of the other patients. While the law might mandate hospital delivery, it couldn't make me stay there afterward. Shortly after Dr. Paul made his morning rounds, I told him that I was checking out, but the staff refused to give me my clothes at first request, so I said, "Okay. I'll wear the hospital gown!" To punish me for checking out early, the doctor insisted on my going home in the ambulance. Between the springless vehicle and pot holes in the road, a wagon would have been more comfortable.

Because of his large hands and long fingers, Bill had difficulty milking so the Guernsey cow had already missed her morning milking. By the time I got home to relieve her, her udder was nearly bursting.

For the record, my hospital stay for Judy was eleven hours, for Audrey seven, and for Tom five.

In spite of our cushy job on the Donovan spread, Bill still was determined to be "his own boss." He located an abandoned farmstead, also Ballard property, closer to Alturas. There was water on the place but no buildings except an open shed and a cellar with a concrete floor. We moved into the cellar and Judy discovered the fun of dropping her glass bottles from her crib and watching them break. I don't know if she was fascinated by the sound effects or the abstract designs created by the spilled milk.

Perhaps the latter as she demonstrated early artistic talent, drawing a credible cat by the time she was two.

Later we converted the shed into a house and acquired a pup, which was allowed to stay indoors until he was big enough to stay outside. The first night that I put him outside, I was awakened by his yelping at the door. I grabbed the broom in my left hand and flashlight in my right, intending to "sweep" him off the step and scold him, but when I opened the door there was a mountain lion crouched over the howling pup. I jabbed the cat with the broom handle and shone the light in its eyes until it finally relinquished its prey and fled into the darkness. The pup scooted inside and hid under the bed, scared, but not seriously injured. Bill slept blissfully through the whole uproar. When I finally got him awake, he scolded me for not waking him up! We hypothesized that the cat was old with bad teeth and unable to catch wild game so it was resorting to domesticated animals. The next day, we reported the incident to Jay Turner in Alturas who had tracking hounds, but it had rained during the night and the dogs were unable to follow the scent.

Like many men, Bill believed that a truck was the sesame to success. He negotiated a new truck deal with Guy Young Motors in Alturas and went commercial. While he waited for the orders to pour in, he planned to cut fire wood and fence posts on the side, a low-income, labor-intensive endeavor at best. Since he liked to dawdle over breakfast coffee and cigarettes until it was too late to go to work, a cash-flow problem was inevitable. Finally I realized that the only solution was to go to work with him, so I bundled up the three little ones and we headed for the tall timber. While he fell and bucked the trees into sixteen or twenty-four inch stove wood, I would split and stack it, but even with us both working, we were barely able to make the truck payments and Interstate Commerce Commission and Public Utility Commission licenses. We had to charge everything else. When I tried to show him the figures in black and red, his comment was, "If that's true, then there's no use working." Before the truck was repossessed, we had one commercial contract: a load of gold ore from the Lost Cabin mine, about twenty-eight miles west of Alturas on the Redding highway, to the smelter in San Francisco for A. K. Wylie, former attorney and now Judge. On another occasion, we scrounged enough scrap iron to make a trip to the foundry in Pittsburgh, California.

One of our clients when we were in the wood business was Charley Watkins, now retired from his many business interests. He still retained a wood yard, which he operated on a commission basis. He clued us in on a four-acre patch of homestead land about nine miles west of Alturas on the back road to Canby. This "open" land was the result of survey error, so we filed a claim. Consisting of sagebrush and juniper, it was fenced on three sides but had no water or structures. Fortunately, our "homesteading" coincided with the dismantling of the Loveness Logging mill in Canby. Loveness was giving away the bunkhouses to get them removed. Bill borrowed a truck and moved two of the 10' by 12' buildings to our new home and positioned them at right angles to each other with a connecting door. We were close enough to the electric power line that hook-up was not a major problem, but to persuade a well-driller to sink a 160' well "on the cuff" was more difficult. Maybe the driller thought that he could always put a lien on the land to collect, which was not true. Only the Internal Revenue Service can attach a homestead.

We still had our Guernsey cow and her heifer calf, Flossie, who resembled her Hereford father. Since it was the wrong time of year for bummer lambs, we went to the Fritz Nozler Auction yard to try to find a feeder pig or calf. The only thing that I could afford was a sickly-looking calf for $9.00. When I got it home, I found out why. The calf had no palate, so it couldn't suckle. By securing a sponge to the nippled bottle to fill the empty space, I enabled the calf to exert enough pressure with its tongue to effect the nursing reflex. The calf not only survived, it thrived. However, I knew that the sponge idea was only a short-term solution. When the calf was weaned, how would it eat hay and chew its cud? I decided to take it back to the Auction yard before I became any more attached to it. I sold it for $27.00, tripling my investment in three weeks. When lambing season started, I picked up some bummers from Mary Wood, who had grazing rights in the area. As far as I could determine, her husband, a Nevada sheepman, was not related to the Wood family who reared me.

Although the livestock provided milk, butter, cottage cheese, and eggs with an occasional fryer, the homestead was not self-sufficient for five people. With little topsoil and limited water, a garden was impractical. Bill worked enough to keep himself in cigarettes and gasoline for the car, an old Plymouth coupe which he had bought from his brother-in-law, Chris Bauman, in Adin, who operated an auto repair shop. I had so many flats with it that the service station gave me discount rates for fixing them!

Of course, Bill was not the only one who tried and failed. I tried to raise mushrooms. Apparently the temperature and humidity was right for seven varieties of wild mushrooms, but the commercial mycelium did not flush.

Although the wolf was always at our door, it was not poverty that precipitated the end of our marriage. When my youngest son, Tom, was born, Dr. Quinn told Bill that I would not survive another pregnancy and recommended that Bill have a vasectomy. Not only would he not have a vasectomy, he refused to use a prophylactic and objected to my using a diaphragm.

Now, I never have accepted medical opinions as gospel, but I knew that *if* anything happened to me, there would be no one to take care of the kids, so I told him that abstinence was the only alternative. He refused to accept that condition and left, but not, of course, without the usual accusations and recriminations. There was another man, blah, blah, . . . There wasn't and never would be.

When he left, it was fall. All the wood that I had was a few left-over knots "too hard to split," but I split them and scrounged brush and wind-fall for fuel. Even if I could have fallen the few junipers, they would have been too green to burn. And it was cold that winter. A glass of water on the bedside stand froze solid. By doubling up in the two beds and sleeping in our clothes, including coats, the kids, aged two, three, and five, and I survived the winter. We were nine miles from town and no transportation, except shank's mare.

Not long after Bill left, the light man cometh to shut off the electricity for non-payment. However, the water was dependent upon an electric pump, so the man returned to headquarters and told the boss to fire him, he wasn't going to shut off my power! So my account was put on "Hold" pending a miracle.

My miracle was a pint-sized teacher at Del Morma school up Canyon Creek. Miss Dalzell commuted from the Niles Hotel in Alturas to the proverbial one-room schoolhouse. One day she stopped by to inquire if I had any school-age children. I told her that Judy would be ready the following year. Being bright and tactful, she asked me if I could "do" her white blouses for her. She wasn't satisfied with her present service. Later she hired me to trace patterns of a jacket that she had designed. Also she passed the word along that I was looking for work. Members of the school board and ranchers, Ida Kinkaid and Bob Mackey, had house-cleaning and ironing for me, but without wheels, it was difficult to work out a schedule. Miss Dalzell would take me as far as the school where Ida or Bob would pick me up when they delivered their kids. I would work until school was out when the parents went to get their kids, and ride home with Miss Dalzell. Because I had taught my kids to respect other people's property my employers had no objection to my bringing the kids with me to work.

Then my old boss, Percy Harris, stopped by to see me. He told me that Art Belding had defaulted on a '41 Ford that he'd bought from P.B. If I wanted it for a hundred bucks to cover paperwork and delinquent registration, he would arrange a payment schedule. He sent me the pink slip and I went to town to retrieve my prize. "As is" meant no ignition key, no battery, no master cylinder, and tires with bubbles of inner tube peeking out through the side walls. Was I dismayed? Of course not. I always welcomed a challenge.

One day, Steve and one of the Sweeney boys and I and the little ones started to hitch-hike to town. Steve and his friend planned to attend the final Hard-Top races of the season. We hadn't walked far when four hunters in a Jeep stopped to give us a lift. When they dropped us off in Alturas, one of them gave each of us a silver dollar. Instead of being my prudent self, I decided to go to the races, too. As we neared the grandstand, the announcer was telling the crowd to hang on to their ticket stubs; there were three door prizes to be given away. As we passed through the gate, I told the kids to take seats near the announcer's stand because I was going to win one of the prizes. When the drawing took place, the first prize was a man's suit. The second prize was a planter-lamp valued at $15.00 and I had the winning number. A neighbor, Luba Reich, offered me ten dollars for it. Sold! Two dollars went to a locksmith for an ignition key and the balance made a down payment on a $12.00 car battery at Coast-to-Coast. As soon as I earned some money for gas, I was in business. Since the vehicle was standard shift, I was able to drive it without brakes for two months, until I could buy a master cylinder, which Steve installed for me.

In October, 1955, I went to work for the Del Morma school district as custodian. The school board gave me the old teacherage for tearing it down and hauling it off. Part of the usable lumber went into improving our house and the scrap went into the stove.

Besides working at the school, I also worked part-time for Anita Paul, Ida Kinkaid, Hallie Tierney, Maude Server, Helene Donovan, Bess Van Horn, Nook Burrell, Marion Mackey, Etta Conlan, Ida Heard, Hattie Sharp, and Mrs. Swanson. In exchange for professional services, I cleaned the office of John Chase, D.D.S., and did Pete Sistok's laundry to pay for plumbing services. In my spare time, I dug a cess pool in solid rock, built fence and added on another room using old railroad ties. I caught up on the utility and feed bills, and added indoor plumbing.

Like Mark Twain said, "It's no disgrace to be poor, but it is to stay that way."

One Christmas I even played Santa. If you want to know the meaning of warm, forget the thermal underwear and don a Santa suit! I thought I'd melt before I could Ho! Ho! Ho! my escape. But I succeeded in confusing my friends as well as my enemies. No one recognized my voice.

After school, Miss Dalzell taught me Gregg shorthand and I bought a used Royal typewriter on time from Amidon Business Machines in Klamath Falls to practice my typing skills.

Every fall, I traded the milk cow's calf to Bill Hagge for winter hay for my cow. On the whole, I was keeping body and soul together when I had an unexpected visitor. Thelma Barker, of Social Services, had heard of my straightened circumstances and had come to sign me up for Welfare benefits. This was a concept foreign to my nature, but I was finally persuaded to accept supplemental aid to dependent children to augment my earned income. In case of illness or accident it would provide a safety net.

In the fall of 1961, I passed the Civil Service examination for a clerical position with the Forest Service in Alturas. Although I scored much higher on the test, I had to start at GS3, because I didn't have a college degree. Since I still needed one unit to get my high school diploma, I took a correspondence course in American History, under the supervision of Francis R. Page, principal of Surprise Valley Union High School.

Like most parents, I was determined to provide my kids with the educational opportunities that I had missed, so fourteen months later I sold the homestead to the Dukes of Alturas through my realtor, Kennon Heard, and moved to Chico, California, where I opened a Day Nursery.

CHAPTER 14

". . . We are such stuff
As dreams are made of, and our little life
Is rounded with a sleep."

> The Tempest, Act IV, Scene I.
> William Shakespeare

Among my clients were Toni, Traci, and Sandra Page; Robert and William Gray; Phillip D. Williams; Richard Lee Bach; and Kelly Marie Jackson, all of whose parents, except Bach, were attending Chico State College.

But as Robert Burns reminds us, our plans "gang aft agley." My kids did not adjust well to the change from rural to urban environment and their grades suffered. This was a contingency for which I was unprepared. While I was trying to cope with this latest challenge, I received a five dollar gift from my second son. Not much, you say. Well, mighty oaks from tiny acorns grow. With this tiny acorn I was able to take the American College Test (ACT) December 27, 1963, and to qualify for admission to Chico State, the following spring, the first step toward a teaching career and financial independence.

It is said that life begins at forty, but for me, it began at forty-four, when I enrolled at Chico State College. This was before Affirmative Action, but with the help of John Otto, Financial Aid Officer, I was soon signed up for various grants and scholarships and twenty hours per week of Work Study at the College library. By taking the maximum number of units allowed per semester and attending summer classes, I was able to complete a five-year program in three and a half years. During this period, I took advantage of the National Defense Student Loan program to borrow $3,300.00, which included the partial loan cancellation privilege ("forgiveness clause" for teaching in "low-income" or "handicapped children" schools). This debt was retired in full in 1977.

To augment the family income, Tom got a job delivering papers for the *Chico Enterprise Record* and the girls found part-time baby-sitting jobs.

After my first two English classes, the instructor suggested that I take a battery of tests for College graduates. I scored in the 99 percentile in English, so I was exempted from lower division English classes, although I did take a comp class from Dr. Nordhus.

While things were coming up roses on the academic front, trouble was brewing on the home front. One fine spring morning in 1966, my fourteen-year-old daughter said that she was not feeling well and would stay home from school. In rummaging around for medicines and other things to make her comfortable while I was gone to classes, I discovered plans for a tryst that day in our home with a boy friend. I notified the boy's parents, and his father declared that he would take care of the matter at his end. My daughter was too emotionally upset by then to go to school, so I let her stay home. My sixteen-year-old daughter had already dropped out of school and was baby-sitting.

A few hours later, I was in Jankunis' class on the Soviet Union, when I was called to the telephone. It was my older daughter, who told me that Audrey had attempted suicide by taking all the pills in sight. When she didn't drop dead immediately, she called her sister and said, "The damn things don't work." I called Menlo Hospital for an ambulance, and took off for home. Although I had twice as far to go, I beat the ambulance. With early warning, prompt evacuation of the stomach contents took care of the physical problem. Her emotional problems were referred to Stewart Bedford, Ph.D., clinical psychologist.

A year later, unknown to me at the time, Audrey's employer, a business woman with three children, turned her on to drugs. Thanks to the over-prescription of diet pills by doctors, they enabled a new class of pushers. Once addicted to "uppers," her clientele became a profitable sideline.

Then in a short-sighted, belt-tightening effort, the Butte County Welfare Department in Oroville decided to terminate my supplemental benefits to Aid for Families with Dependent Children. Such action at that time would automatically terminate my college education as well. When I showed the notification to John Otto, he said, "Appeal it. I'll help." Lennis Dunlap, English department, and David W. Lantis, geography professor, also agreed to help. As a Junior with a 3.6 grade point average, I was within a year of obtaining my secondary English credential. Thanks to the letters of commendation and support by Otto, Dunlap, and Lantis, the Directors of the Welfare Board reconsidered their decision and extended the grant until I graduated.

On December 12, 1966, I joined Kappa Delta Pi, an honor Society in Education, membership in which is based on academic excellence. On March 12, 1967, sixteen of the top students of the graduating seniors were honored by President Robert E. Hill at the Chico State mansion. I was chosen to represent the English department.

Since a college degree usually includes a personality profile, mine was "interpreted" as "disgustingly normal" by Dr. Hugh M. Bell, Professor of Psychology and Faculty Grand Marshal. Considering that I am the mother of five children, I rated rather low in femininity, not particularly social by nature, nor status conscious. Inventory scores notwithstanding my self-concept has always been very healthy. The humility is purely affective.

Following Commencement exercises, while I was busy looking for a teaching contract and taking summer classes in geology and Adolescent Psychology, I received a letter from my friend and mentor, Kathleen Dalzell. She was suing a dentist in Seattle, Washington, for malpractice and she wanted me to testify as a character witness at her jury trial July 10, 1967. Naturally I was happy to have an opportunity to repay some of her kindness and help, but I doubted that she would win her case. Testimonials are a poor substitute for hard evidence, and there wasn't any. Just her word against his. Lorena Northrup also testified for Kathleen, but it was a waste of time and money. Later we heard that the local dental association had limited their colleague's practice to making dentures, a partial victory for the victim's side.

Before Kathleen's case, I had appeared as a character witness for Roberta Penner in a divorce action.

But my education really began when I walked into my classroom at Bishop Union High School in Bishop, California. Some thirty ninth graders were leapfrogging over desks and dictionaries were flying through the air like confetti. According to class management courses, one waited until the students settled down before introducing one's self, taking roll, etc. If I had followed this advice, I would have turned into a pillar of salt like Lot's wife. While I was deciding on an alternative course of control, someone from the office delivered the class roster. When the door opened, the class "settled" temporarily. It could have been the Superintendent of Schools, George Alexson. Of course, the roster was no help. The kids "swapped names," responding to a different name on any given day. Try to achieve a "seating arrangement" under those conditions. To further confuse the issue, most ninth graders look alike, particularly boys, all ears, noses, and elbows, generally shorter than the girls, and all dressed in the "uniform" of the latest fad.

However, the most disconcerting part was that I became "the enemy" the moment I took my position in front of the class, which was a complete reversal of my former rapport with kids of all ages. With few exceptions, my hundred and fifty students were openly hostile and dedicated to misbehavior. One of my predecessors, a man, had been dangled from the second-story window by some of the students to teach him a lesson. One of my students had been rescued the previous year from being hanged by his classmates by the timely intervention of a custodian. I was also informed that the district employed two full-time glaziers for damage control. Nor was I the only target of their mischief. In Mr. Anderson's class, the students sawed the legs off desks and otherwise entertained themselves.

One of the exceptions in my class was Darla Frenzi who wrote the following poem for me:

Teachers

"We are but blind, lost sheep,
Who have no place to sleep,

Those teachers - hated by all,
Never quit or let us fall.

Remember they didn't have to teach,
And they didn't have to preach.

They wanted to; yes, they wanted to.
They wanted to teach me and you.

We are the lost sheep in the night,
They are the shepherds to lead us to light."

126

These were not inner-city kids, minorities, culturally or economically deprived. Bishop, service center for an estimated 7,000 population, is District headquarters for California Division of highways, Interstate Telephone Company, Southern California Edison Company, Los Angeles Department of Water and Power, etc. Although Bishop is adjacent to a Paiute Reservation, only two or three of my students were Native Americans. Except for poor attendance they were never a behavior problem.

At Parents' Night, I was surprised to see mostly fathers. One, a dentist, discussed his son's poor grades and asked my opinion. I told him that the boy was too busy "goofing off" to perform up to his potential. The father thanked me, and after the Christmas holidays, the boy started earning "A"s and "B"s instead of "C"s and "D"s. Apparently, he had spent his holiday washing dishes at Mammoth Ski Resort as a lesson in "uneducated" employment options. Too bad more parents don't share that father's wisdom.

One of the few bright spots in my memories of that year was Dan Chitty, who managed to achieve academic excellence and still avoid the stigma of egg-head with his peers, no mean feat.

My final hour in that classroom was my finest. The Superintendent had warned the teachers that classes had walked out "early" on the last day of school in the past, and he did not want this to happen this year. Being forewarned, I gradually gravitated toward the exit several minutes before the dismissal bell was programmed to ring. I was in front of the closed door, when the class rose and the ring-leader, an overgrown bully, announced that they were leaving. When he repeated his threat, I said, "Over my dead body." He blinked, and his eyes flickered. Apparently no one had ever faced up to him before, and he didn't know how to back down without "losing face." Finally he said, "Then we'll go out the window." The window was two stories above the paved walk. Since I could not defend two exits at once, I decided to try reverse psychology, often effective with males. "Go ahead," I said.

"You mean you don't *care*?" responded a chorus of awed voices. For the first time that year, I had their undivided attention. As I looked from face to face, I asked, "Why should I?" The proverbial pin dropping would have sounded like the crack of doom in the tomb-like silence. They were still frozen in tableau when the bell rang. I opened the door and stood aside, as they quietly filed out and marched down the stairs still mute.

Needless to say, the teacher turnover was very high. Of the five replacement teachers hired the previous fall, only two stayed on, one of whom had ten years experience and taught an elective.

After my first tour of duty in the combat zone of secondary education, I questioned my choice of careers. I wanted to teach, not police a mass of hormones. So I took a sabbatical from teaching and sought blue-collar employment, where I discovered that I was now "overqualified" and found temporary jobs in a convalescent home and as dishwasher at the Sundown Restaurant in Chico.

Of course, every cloud has a silver lining, and I was ecstatic when I was notified that my appointment to the position of Clerical Assistant 1-A at Chico State College Library was confirmed, effective April 1, 1969. Beginning salary was $2.18 per hour. This serendipitous state of affairs lasted eight months, when Governor Reagan's budgetary belt-tightening resulted in the termination of sixteen new employees at the library. The Reagan budget was a Hydra-headed monster: the more he cut, the larger it became, the largest in California history.

By October, it was too late to apply for a teaching position, so I did some substitute teaching and in March of 1970 I became part-time care attendant for Margaret Frazier, twenty-one hours a week at $1.65 per hour.

After two years in the "over-qualified" market, I was ready to give teaching another whirl, using my own class management techniques. I accepted a position in Dayville, Oregon, a small community in Grant County north of John Day. The base pay was $7,000.00 per annum.

Besides secondary English, I taught Journalism, Art, Speech and Drama, and pinch-hit as librarian, yearbook advisor and play director.

South of Dayville was Rothwell's Boys Ranch, an organization for delinquent boys, seven of whom were enrolled in my classes. One of them posed the first challenge to my authority by stretching his leg out in the aisle to block my passage. I stopped and said quietly, "Please move your foot." And waited. I didn't repeat myself nor threaten. Just waited, while the class watched to see who would blink first. As the silence dragged on, the boy finally pulled his foot back under his desk, and tried to save face by saying innocently, "Oh, was my foot in your way?" I continued with my interrupted explanation of class rules: 1) common garden variety courtesy, to classmates as well as to the teacher, i.e., do not interrupt when another is speaking; 2) although gum-chewing was *verboten* by school policy, students in my class had a choice: they could chew and not talk, or talk and not chew. Since everyone wanted to talk, they chucked their gum in a waste basket as they entered my room; 3) the only four-letter word not allowed in my classroom was "can't." I also individualized instruction for a variety of reasons. I soon discovered that "going by the book" resulted in one or two students doing the work and sharing it. By offering a choice of study, the student was more interested and committed to his task, whether it was spelling, grammar, punctuation, creative writing, criticism, outlines, poetry, etc., and the student was working at his own level, not competing. This approach was highly successful and popular. What did I care if a boy wanted to "do" motorcycles as long as he learned to do outlines, research, footnotes, bibliography, and the mechanics of encoding simultaneously?

My Journalism class was so popular that all of the students signed up for it, not just the academically elite, so I initiated a program which combined reading, current events, and cartooning. Each student would read and illustrate a newspaper article. Our classroom walls became a "movie" of history in the making.

The only useful teaching tip that I learned in college was "never lecture to a pre-college level class. The academically oriented already know it and are bored, and the others tune it out." Many teachers are so impressed with their own erudition and the sound of their own voices that they waste the whole period lecturing and then have to assign homework (which is done by family and friends, if at all) to have something to grade.

I told my class that if they worked during my classes, we would skip the homework. They worked like beavers. The only good thing that can be said of homework is that it challenges the creativity of the student to produce excuses for not doing it.

After the preliminary roll call and return of corrected papers, I would announce the assignment and tell them to get busy. As soon as someone realized that he/she didn't understand and asked for help, I would use the Socratic method of asking questions to lead the student to discover the answer for him/her self. The "Eureka" principle of Archimedes is a powerful reinforcement to learning.

Although relevance was the by-word of the '60's and '70's, relevance is still the key to education. By relating math a "macho" subject, to poetry, a "sissy" one, I was able to dispel old prejudice and empower a whole class of poets.

I bided my time until I overheard a boy remark that poetry was "sissy stuff." I said, "Anyone who can count can write poetry." The young man promptly challenged me to "prove it."

I started with cinquain, counting words arranged in the following format:

Leaves   (1 word)
Red, gold   (2 modifiers)
Flying, frisking, falling   (3 participles)
Through the frosty air   (4 word phrase)
Leaves   (1 word refrain)

Then we moved on to counting syllables in Haiku which features a single image, about nature, in the present tense, limited to seventeen syllables, divided into three lines (5-7-5).

Rushes in the pond
Standing in rapt attention
Salute the morning.

After that, we counted stress patterns, the repetition of which accounted for the rhythm in poetry and music. Translating these stress patterns into poetic feet called iambs, trochees, anapests, dactyls, and spondees seemed to come naturally. Once it was demonstrated that poetry could be quantified like a mathematical equation or chemical formula, it no longer posed a problem for the macho types. For the rest of that quarter, all my students spent their free time period in my room writing poetry!

At last I was teaching and enjoying it. However, a problem was developing on another front. Some of my students complained that the lunch period was too short; they did not have time to eat and to make a pit stop. When the complaints escalated, I agreed to check it out. Oregon law specified a thirty-minute lunch break and ours was only twenty. I reported this discrepancy to the superintendent, Mr. Meserole. He agreed to take care of it. Nothing happened, so I brought up the subject again at a faculty meeting. Again Meserole promised to correct the problem, but nothing changed. He also censored the contents of our weekly paper, the *Tenderfoot,* finally declaring that there was no more paper available. I volunteered to supply the necessary paper and he said that he would not allow it. He definitely did not believe in the people's right to know what was happening on campus. Later he posted "no trespassing" signs on the perimeter of the school grounds and physically tried to restrain a board member from coming on campus. To make a long story short, Mr. Meserole's employment was terminated for inefficiency, insubordination, mental incapacity, neglect of duty, etc. In spite of his dismissal, he refused to vacate his office and had to be physically removed by officers. The trial of Russell J. Meserole *vs* School District 16-J was resolved in favor of the District November 30, 1970. Lawrence Wolfgram, science teacher, was appointed interim superintendent.

That fall, I entered the *Tenderfoot* in the Columbia Scholastic Press Association competition for the best high school paper. It took fourth prize in its class nationwide, and I won a Journalism Fellowship Award and a scholarship to the Regional Newspaper Fund Institute at California State University, Fulleron, California, the following summer.

Since the *Tenderfoot* also reached its golden anniversary that year, I organized a reunion for former *Tenderfoot* staff. Former members came from as far away as Arizona, Florida, New Jersey, and Canada. We printed an abridged history of the paper and its journalistic success. In 1922, the infant publication placed first in the state, and took first prize in the national CSPA in 1929 and 1932, and second in 1931 and 1933. In 1930, it won a silver loving cup for the best mimeograph paper in Oregon. I was proud to be a part of its continuing tradition of excellence.

The Newspaper Institute in Fulleron lasted three weeks, and one day was spent touring the major media offices and studios in Los Angeles. This tour coincided with L.A.'s first smog alert of the year.

Although I enjoyed my teaching experience in Dayville, my home was in Chico, so I did not renew my contract in Oregon.

However, there were still about one hundred English teachers for every position so I wound up baby-sitting for Diana Lloyd and Linda Brashears in Chico, doing home care for Erma Ward in Yuba City until she was hospitalized with her thirteenth heart attack, and baby-sitting for Milton Jeffries in Marysville.

With my three kids "finding themselves" elsewhere, I had a spare room at my disposal, so I signed up with California Youth Authority for Foster Home Care. That was a very short-lived venture. The young man had psychological problems, like masturbating in public, with which I was not qualified to deal. I even tried renting the room, but that too proved untenable.

Then I received a telephone call from Clara Eddie, Superintendent of Schools for Modoc County. My friend and former teacher, Jesse Lee Arkarro, had told her that I was looking for a teaching job, and Clara had an opening in Special Education. I pointed out that my credential was for secondary English and geography. She said that I could teach on a provisional basis until I secured a Special Ed. credential under the Fisher Bill. Three days later I reported for duty in Alturas.

Modoc County also provided Special Services (teachers, psychologists, speech therapists, school nurse, etc.) to the Tulelake Basin Joint Unified schools, so I was transferred to Newell the following year. In Newell, I discovered that the Special Ed. students had been completely segregated from the "normal" population at all times, including the cafeteria, playgrounds, even the halls. Fortunately, Newell also had a new principal, Ron Mullanix, who supported my efforts to "integrate" my class into the general population. The irony of this Neanderthal policy was that these kids were neither severely retarded nor had behavior problems, just slow learners, dyslexic, or abused. I thought that I had overcome the local prejudice until the eighth grade graduation, when one of my students, who had passed the State required tests, was not included in the list of graduates and no seat provided for him on stage. I promptly requested a correction for the oversight, and Gary Malone took his rightful place with the other grads. Not only had they been socially ostracized, but their curriculum was limited to "survival skills" like tying their shoe laces (even though laceless shoes and boots have been around for ages) and candle-making. Reading was restricted to bathroom and traffic signs.

Since I still hear frequent gripes from school cooks about the "waste" of government subsidized food, I suggest trying Mullanix's solution when the Newell cooks complained to him about the problem. He came into the cafeteria during lunch period and told the reluctant diners that they were free to go play as soon as their trays were "clean." Maybe they did gobble their food, but they didn't waste any more of it. True this policy meant longer playground duty for teachers, but nothing's perfect.

Nor did I blame the new policy when I got chilled and developed double pneumonia, but I did buy a warmer coat when I recovered, just in case.

The next eight and a half years, I taught Special Ed. without tenure. In this respect, I think that the policy of accountability is far superior to the unaccountability of tenured teachers. Voters get "steamed" about term limits for government representatives, even though the elected official has to "renew his contract" with the public every two, four, or six years. A teacher hangs on for the three-year probationary period and has a lifetime license "to be or not to be" a conduit of knowledge until retirement. A case in point was a fourth grade teacher I met in a science class. She maintained that the sun was a planet. She had been teaching her pupils that for twenty years and wasn't about to change because some jumped-up college professor said differently. I know many middle-aged teachers who are still using their original lesson plans. Why not? There is no incentive to change, to grow, to improve. While the argument that the text does not change is basically true, the students do, and the material must be constantly adapted to meet the changing conditions. Teaching "by the book" has probably been responsible for more "drop-outs" than any other single factor. During my student teaching, one of my master teachers, who was nearing retirement, first had me "observe" from the back of the classroom, before taking over as teacher. As she read the dry-as-dust questions at the end of each chapter of the text, I watched as boredom, then alternative activities, took over the class. "How old was so-and-so?" Who cared? What difference did it make? The answer required minimum recall and no thinking.

One student was particularly frustrated with this superficial treatment of the story and was borderline expulsion or drop-out. When I gravitated to the front of the class, I asked "why" questions, which stimulated challenging discussions of the historical significance of the events in the story. Another incident also highlighted my different approach to teaching. I intercepted a note from one girl to another and placed it on the lectern until the end of class. As the students were leaving, I called the girl up to my desk and handed the note to her. "But you didn't read it," she exclaimed. "Why should I? It wasn't mine. Just pass notes on your own time in the future, not mine, Okay?" Later I learned that many teachers saved these silly missives and preserved them in the student's permanent files. Invasion of privacy isn't my bag.

A few years later when I was on CSC campus for summer school, I was passing the Bell Memorial Union en route to class. A tall, lanky young man unfolded himself from the steps where he had been sitting with a lovely blonde girl and threw his arms around me. "Mrs. Edwards," he exclaimed, "without you I would have flunked or dropped out of school. Thanks to you, I finished high school and am now a teaching assistant in the Music department here at the College!" Talk about music to my ears!

"Ricardo! How wonderful!" He introduced his girl friend and we caught up on mutual news. His testimonial was the kind that any teacher would treasure.

In the early seventies, I took advantage of Greyhound's bargain tour package to see the U.S. of A. and to visit my son in Massachusetts. From the Mormon tabernacle in Salt Lake City, to Washington, D.C., that still showed the ravages of racial unrest, to Philadelphia that "dripped with history," to the Big Apple with its aura of boundless energy, to New Hampshire with its post-card scenery, to Boston with its cobbled streets, and north to Quebec, west to Toronto, Ontario, and back to Detroit via the tunnel between Lake Erie and Lake Huron, I followed the itinerary with which I was already familiar through the pages of history and literature. I must concede that Canadian buses are more elegant and comfortable than their American counterparts and faster. We cruised along at 80 mph and never stopped at railroad crossings. On my second tour, I did the Pacific Northwest, sandwiched in between summer sessions and teaching schedules.

CHAPTER 15

"Life's but a walking shadow; a poor player,
That struts and frets his hour upon the stage,
And then is heard no more: it is a tale
told by an idiot, full of sound and fury,
Signifying nothing."

Macbeth, Act V, Scene IV
William Shakespeare

During the Thanksgiving holidays in 1976, I managed to slip and fall, wedging my left ankle between a vehicle and the curb, resulting in total displacement of the foot and multiple broken bones. I heard four of them snap. Fortunately, the accident occurred within blocks of the Rideout Hospital in Marysville. After two hours of surgery and seven days in the hospital, I returned to Tulelake, but did not return to the classroom until after New Year's. Unable to master crutches, I taught the spring semester in a wheel chair.

Never being happy paying rent, I bought a fixer-upper on Modoc Avenue in January 1978, and sank $25,000 into remodeling it. I did most of the carpentering myself and some of the electrical wiring. Only in my old age have I tackled plumbing! The remodeling was part of my retirement plan. Having entered the teaching profession late (age 47), I figured that I would need supplemental income to augment my pension. By adding another bedroom, bath, and family room, I could operate a Day Care center in my home. Of course, by the time I took early retirement in 1982, exorbitant insurance premiums and state regulations rendered day-care too expensive for the low-income families.

Besides teaching and carpentering, I served on two juries, one for alleged poaching and another for Use of Excessive Force by a teacher in disciplining a student. Both defendants were found not guilty.

Soon after retirement, time and money became a problem: too much of the former and not enough of the latter. So I took a part-time job with the Senior Citizen's Community Service as a trainee at the USDA, Forest Service, at Doublehead Ranger Station. When that ended, I enrolled with Green Thumb, serving as a part-time teacher's aid. After three years with Green Thumb, I sold my place to James Lee and moved to Oakland where I went to work as administrative assistant to Ann Rankin, attorney. While in Oakland, I renewed my search for my brother, Gene. As usual, I was too late. He had died February 20, 1967, in Oakland of diabetic ketoacidosis and bronco-pneumonia. He was buried in the Golden Gate National Cemetery.

Ten months later, Lee defaulted, and I returned to Tulelake.

In July, 1988, I became a Volunteer in Service to America (VISTA), offering literacy and English as a second language classes in my home. I also worked with the Immigration and Naturalization Service during their Amnesty program for resident aliens. During the three years as a VISTA, I found time to take a correspondence course in tax preparation and to be licensed and bonded by the State. Of course, I couldn't charge for my services while on the VISTA payroll, and by then H.& R. Block, *et al*, were issuing instant tax refunds. Always a day late and a dollar short.

In July 1991, I sold my place to Maria Campos and moved to Yuba City in search of a milder climate. There I continued as a VISTA for La Familia, a non-profit adult-education organization dedicated to literacy. Rudy De La Cerna was executive director. Most of the target population was Hispanic with Hmong, Thai, Lao, and Punjabi running a close second. Many of these enrollees, who were receiving public assistance, admitted that they could get minimum wage jobs, but because there was no medical benefits included for their families, they opted to stay on welfare. But my most memorable students were a few Afghan ladies who wanted to learn to speak the King's English because they realized that being able to communicate in the host language of their new home was the key to social and financial success.

In the fall, I became a "loaned executive" to the Yuba-Sutter United Way Campaign, 1991-92, the primary objective of which was to consolidate community fund-raising efforts of twenty-four service organizations under one umbrella. Thanks to my efforts, La Familia's allocation was increased by $2,000.00. and I was awarded a quartz digital clock with my name etched in gold.

When my VISTA tour ended, I decided to move back to God's country with mountains and trees, away from the respiratory problems that plagued me in the valley.

My last public service was as a part-time receptionist for Great Northern Corporation in Weed, California. At 72, I retired again. However, I was soon complaining about "nothing to do," so two of my friends, Janet Ice and Barbara Brittain, suggested that I write the story of my life. Since my recall was not infallible, I decided to document everything and to research the genealogies of both my families; my "real" parents and my surrogate parents.

In the following reconstruction of my heritage, based on historical documents, I shall begin with the Heald lineage, since my mother was Eleanor Florence Heald, the youngest of five children born to Francis Fletcher Heald and Laura Anna Heald, née Paxton.

CHAPTER 16

"Methinks my moiety, north of Burton here,
In quantity equals not one of yours:
See how this river comes me cranking in
And cuts me from the best of all my land
A huge half-moon, a monstrous cantle out."

King Henry IV, Part I, Act III, Scene I.
William Shakespeare

Today Berwick-on-Tweed, Northumberland, is part of the boundary between England and Scotland, but in 1615 when my great, great ancestor, John Heald, was born, the border was still in dispute. King James I of England (also known as James IV of Scotland), son of Mary, Queen of Scots, had succeeded Elizabeth I to the throne. Between the political power struggle and religious reformation, the British Isles were in almost constant turmoil. During this unsettled period, John Heald migrated south and west to Alderley, Cheshire, England, where he met and married Dorothy Royle. Their first three children, Hannah (August 14, 1635), John, Jr., (December 3, 1636), and Timothy, 1638, were born in Alderley. Before John Heald emigrated to America in 1641, he was granted the Crest and Coat of Arms shown on the following page.[98]

HEALD

*John Heald, from Berwick, Northumb, England,
to Concord, Mass., 1635.*

HEALD

John Heald, from Berwick, Northumb.,
  Eng., to Concord, Mass., 1635.

Arms—Argent, on a chevron gules, betw.
  three bombs sable fired ppr., as many
  bezants; a chief of the second.

Crest—A sword and key in saltire ppr.

From: *Armoury and Blue Book* by Mathews, Vol. 2, page
103, published in London, 1908. (Also check *General
Armory* by William Armstrong Crozier.)

Arriving in America, he became one of the twelve founders of
Concord, Middlesex County, Massachusetts, where Dorcas (March 22,
1645), Gershom (March 23, 1647), Dorothy (August 16, 1649), Thomas
(January 19, 1651), and Israel (July 30, 1660) were born.

In 1662, John Heald died, leaving his wife, Dorothy, and eight
children. The following is a typed copy of his last will and testament:

"The Will . . . of . . . John Heald (1615-1662)
From: Berwick-on-Tweed, 1631-35
Freeman: 1641

I, John Heald of Concord in County of Middlesex in Massachusetts Collony, being sick in body but of perfect mind and
memory, I do make this my last will and testament in manner
and form following: first I commit my soule into the hands of
the Lord my gratious God in Jesus Christ resting upon his free

grace (?) that he will receive it —- and my body to the earth to be decently buryed therein; believing the resurrection thereof at the Last Day, and hoping that both soule and body shall be glorified together with my blessed redeemer forever; Also for the outward estate which God hath given me; my three eldest children that is to say John my eldest son, and Timothy and my daughter Hannah having received their portions of my estate; I do hereby give and bequeth to my five younger children; to each of them the sum of thirteen (13?) pounds six shillings and eight pence to be payed unto the said children by my loving wife Dorothy or her assigns (?) when the foresaid children shall come to the age of twenty and one years or at their marriage; and the rest of my estate be it more or less I do hereby give it to my said wife to dispose of as she shall think good excepting one (?) suit of cloaths which I give to my eldest son John, and my great coat to my son Timothy; and a wastcoat to my daughter Hannah; Also I do hereby appoint and constitute my said beloved wife Dorothy, the sole executrix of this my last will and testament.

In wittnes whereof I doe herto set my hand and seal this ninteenth day of Aprill one thousand six hundred sixty two.

(signed) John Heald
Wittnesses hereof
John Flynt (Signed)
Ephraim Flynt "
Thomas Brown "
     Attested, Simon Willard (Signed)
     Entered June 18 1662 Thomas Danforth
    Inventory   May 31, 1662 shows
              Estate of 141 lbs - 1 shilling and debts
                  of 1 lb to be paid
            Net estate of 140 -I
              (Signed) Robert Merriam, George
Wheeler,
             Thomas Brooks, ...
             (Could not read the rest)."[99]

Captain Simon Willard, one of the signers of the foregoing document, became a "chiefe instrument in erecting this town,"[100] and the leader "of the band of Concord [militia]."[101]

Another witness, Thomas Danforth, was one of the thirty-seven members of the Council of Safety and signer of "the Declaration of the Gentlemen, Merchants and Inhabitants of Boston and Country Adjacent (4-18-1689)"[102] and later became deputy governor under Governor Andros.[103]

John Heald's daughter, Hannah, married John Spaulding; John Heald, Jr., married Sarah Frances Dane (Dean); Timothy wed Sarah Barber; Dorcas (no record); Gershom espoused Ann Vinton; Dorothy wed John Fletcher, grandson of Robert Fletcher, who migrated to Concord, Massachusetts in 1630.; Thomas Heald chose Priscilla Markham as his wife, and Israel married Martha Wright.[104]

Robert Fletcher's relative, Moses Fletcher, had arrived on the *Mayflower*, but he died the first year.

During the Revolutionary War, John Heald, IV, and his son, Oliver Heald, and his brother, Ephraim Heald, Sr., were Minutemen. John's son, Israel, was a Captain as was Timothy Heald, III, and Josiah Heald's son, Samuel.[105]

Although records are incomplete, my research has convinced me that my maternal grandfather, Francis Fletcher Heald, is a descendant of the John Heald family tree. Besides Dorothy Heald's marriage to John Fletcher, there were several Heald-Fletcher unions: Dorcas Heald married William Fletcher January 28, 1734; Samuel Heald wed Rebecca Fletcher; Oliver Heald espoused Esther Fletcher; Dorothy Heald, III, married Joshua Fletcher. In fact, the Fletcher name appears no less than sixty-five times in the first five generations of the John Heald genealogy and not once in the Samuel Heald branch. Based on the "circumstantial evidence" of the Fletcher name and his Vermont heritage, I believe that grandfather's lineage to John Heald has been established.

In 1703, Samuel Heald, son of William and Jane Donbabin Heald, of Mobberley, Cheshire, England, settled in Chester County, Pennsylvania. Samuel was a Quaker and a collateral branch of the Heald family tree. One of his descendants, Emma Hale (Heald), became the wife of Joseph Smith, Mormon prophet.[106] Joseph Smith was the "son of a poor New England farmer . . . [who] had a vision that led him to dig up golden plates covered with sacred writings. Translated by him, they were published as the *Book* of Mormon."[107] However, hostility toward the practice of polygamy led to his imprisonment and death by a lynch mob in 1844.

Because of the general mispronunciation of the name *Heald* /Hailed/ and the tendency to "swallow" final "d's," Heald frequently becomes Hale, much to the confusion of genealogical researchers.

The most prominent Heald in the Bay area was Edward Payson Heald, founder of Heald's Business Colleges. He was born February 5, 1841, in Lovell, Oxford County, Maine, one of twelve children born to Abel and Mary Heald. His twin, Edwin A., died young.[108]

He arrived in San Francisco by sailing ship from Maine in 1862 at the age of nineteen, and started his college the following year. During the earthquake in 1906, while Giannini was rescuing the flammable assets of Bank of America in a wheelbarrow, Heald was burying twenty-four Remington typewriters in Union Square. Two weeks later he reopened the College in his home on Franklin Street.

Professor Heald was also a member of the Pacific Coast Trotting Horse Breeders' Association in Sonoma County and took many prizes at State and County Fairs.

He died July 11, 1925, at his home, 3207 Telegraph Avenue in Oakland. He was survived by his widow, Rowena Heald, his youngest brother, Reverend Josiah Heald, El Paso, Texas, nephews Joe Heald of Los Angeles and Edward H. Stearns of Chicago, and niece, Mrs. C. Purington, of Los Angeles.[109]

Grandfather Francis Fletcher Heald was born March 29, 1864, in San Francisco. On December 10, 1864, his future spouse, Laura Anna Paxton, was born to Robert and Anna Meacham Paxton in Virginia City, Nevada. Originally from Ohio, they joined the gold rush to the "rude little settlement called Ophir Diggings" which was to become the metropolitan mining camp of Virginia City.[110] Robert and Annie Paxon (sic) appeared on the Nevada 1860 Territorial Census Index and Robert Paxton was listed in the First Directory of Nevada Territory in 1862 as miner, living on the West side of A Street, opposite Sutton Avenue. This address was next door to the newspaper, *The Territorial Enterprise*, situated at the corner of A Street and Sutton Avenue, the business section of Virginia City.[111]

Since Samuel Clemens was writing for the *Enterprise* under the pen name, Josh, during this period, it is highly likely that my great grandfather and "Josh" were acquainted. On Groundhog's Day, 1863, Josh changed his pen name to Mark Twain.[112]

According to the 1860 Census, the population in Virginia City was 2,345 (139 females) with forty-two saloons, forty-two general stores, nine doctors, one dentist, two teachers, one milliner, a preacher and zero lawyers. Three years later the population was 15,000 and "the streets were literally paved with silver. The ore was assorted into grades. The richest, $1,000 a ton, was sacked for shipment to England. The second and third classes were piled aside for future milling. Any ore assaying less than $50.00 a ton was used to pave "A," "B," and "C," Streets."[113]

Robert Paxton figured prominently in the mining records in the Inventory and Index of the Carson County, Utah, and Nevada Territories, 1855-61.

Mining—	Robert Paxton and Alexander E. O'Neil to John O. Earl mining claim S. of Ophir, interest in Gould ground in Rogers & Co. in Virginia City. Bill of sale recorded 12-14-1859. Book 1, pp. 121-2.
Mining—	Paxton and O'Neil to Earl - interest in Caldwell lead between Gold Hill and Virginia City. pp. 266-268.
Mining—	R. R. Beach to Robert Paxton -Choctaw Claim. pp. 73-4.
Mining—	M. C. Hillyer to Herman C. Leonard-interest acquired through Robert Paxton in Flowery District. pp. 143-44.
Real Estate—	Robert Paxton to Justin Howard - land in Virginia City. pp. 56-57.
Mining—	Paxton and O'Neil to David Orean and F. R. Miller 50' of Norman Company's Lake Star lead S. of Six-mile Canyon. pp. 175-76. Abrogation of Notice: Robert Paxton and John F. Sabins. Revoke notice of mining claim struck by Stewart and Kirkpatrick south of Gold Hill. Notice of same filed in favor of Robert Paxton and A. J. Brown. pp. 793-94.
Mining—	Paxton to H. T. Templeton 50' in Milton Co. in Gold Hill District. pp. 43-44.

Mining—   A. D. Brown and Robert Paxton to James G. Dow and James A. Butler. Also interest in Milton Lode in Gold Hill District. pp. 354-5.

Mining—   Paxton and Brown to P. C. Cust. Interest in Milton claim. p. 54.

Survey—   Paxton and Sabins 165' of quartz lode. p. 103.

John O. Earl was one of the incorporators of the Ophir Management Company organized April 28, 1860, with $5,040,000 and 16,800 shares, and President of the Gould and Curry Bonanza.[114]

M. C. Hillyer was a notable Comstock Mine Superintendent at Siver Hill.[115]

The aforementioned Gould "sold his claim for $450.00 to George Hearst and lived out his days running a peanut stand in Reno."[116]

Because of the disastrous fire in October 1875, when a "sea of fire swept down 'C' Street, two thousand buildings burned, ten million dollars lost" and most records were destroyed.[117] Without these records, I can only conjecture that great grandmother, Annie Paxton, died in childbirth, and infant Laura Anna Paxton was reared by her aunt Elvira Meacham. At fifteen Laura Paxton, niece of Elvira Meacham, was living on Natoma Street in San Francisco.[118]

Robert Paxton, miner, appears in the Elko, Nevada, 1870 Census with no family.

The loss of the 1890 Census records to fire and the San Francisco earthquake in 1906 have compounded the difficulty in documenting when my maternal grandparents met and married, but I do have their wedding photos. My mother, Eleanor Florence Heald, was born in Edmonds, Washington, August 12, 1901, the youngest of five children and the only girl.

In the summer of 1917, my mother met Charles Henry Tendering, a Marine stationed at the Mare Island Naval Base in Vallejo, California. Although he was born November 8, 1890, in Seattle, Washington, to Charles Henry and Hedwig Koster Tendering, he was living in St. Paul, Minnesota, when he enlisted. Even though born in America, my father's German heritage was the focus of the strong anti-German prejudice dominating the country since the outbreak of World War I. For this reason and my mother's youth, not yet sixteen, they did not broadcast their

Francis Fletcher Heald,
b. March 29, 1864
(San Francisco, Ca.),
d. June 18, 1946.

Laura Anna Paxton,
b. Dec. 10, 1864
(Virginia City, Nev.),
d. April 18, 1942.

Charles Henry Tendering,
b. Nov. 8, 1890 (Seattle, Wa.),
m. Jan. 21, 1918
(Eleanor Florence Heald),
d. July 21, 1935 (Holtville, Ca.).

Elizabeth Maxine Tendering,
b. Nov. 1, 1919 (Portland, Or.)
Charles Eugene Tendering,
b. March 17, 1918,
d. Feb. 20, 1967 (Oakland, Ca.).

romance. In fact, she was seven months pregnant before her family discovered her condition. One of the reasons that there were few unwed mothers in the good old days was a tradition called "shotgun weddings." This process not only legitimized the offspring but fixed responsibility for support simultaneously. While the "shotgun" may have been figurative in nature, it was no less effective. On January 21, 1918, Charles H. Tendering and Eleanor F. Heald were married in the First Baptist Church in San Francisco by Arthur H. Gordon, Minister of the Gospel. Fellow Marine, Jack W. Hedrick, was a witness. After the ceremony, the new bride was ordered to never darken her parents' door again, and even her name was banned from the family vocabulary.

On March 17, 1918, my brother, Charles Eugene Tendering, was born. Having been reared in an affluent home with doting parents and indulgent older brothers, my mother was ill-prepared to cope on the forty-dollar a month allotment that she received from the Government.

A few months after the Armistice, November 11, 1918, my father requested a discharge from the U.S.M.C. so that he could better support his wife and son. When his request was unanswered, C. F. Curry, House of Representatives, Washington, D.C., wrote to Major General George Barnett, Commandant.[119]

In response, the Major General reminded Representative Curry that Private Tendering had enlisted for four years . . . and discharges of four-year men were considered only in extreme cases. Apparently, my father's case did not qualify as extreme.

As mentioned earlier, I was born November 1, 1919, in Portland, Oregon.

On October 27, 1920, my father won First Prize ($20.00) in the Small Arms and Gunnery competition as a marksman in Olalla, Washington. On February 2, 1921, he re-enlisted, and three months later my mother sued him for desertion although he was still on duty in the Corps! The child support allotment was terminated July 27, 1922, because Gene and I were in the custody of our grandmother, Laura Heald.

Sometime during this chaotic period, my mother produced a third child, a half-brother named Tommy, who was adopted by a doctor in the Bay area.

After a tour of duty in Olongapo and Cavite, The Philippines, my father was given a medical transfer back to Mare Island, followed by an

C. F. CURRY
3D DISTRICT CALIFORNIA

Navy-dis-Lendering, Pvt. C H USMC M7-I
CFC-jp

House of Representatives U. S.

Washington, D. C.

September
Twentieth
1 9 1 9

Major General George Barnett,
Commandant, U. S. Marine Corps,
Navy Department,
Washington.

My dear General:

I am informed that Private Charles H. Lendering, Marine Barracks, Navy Yard, Mare Island, California, made an application for discharge and filed it with his Commanding Officer on May 8, 1919. However, he is still in the Service and has heard nothing from it.

Private Lendering is married and has a child, both living in Woodland, California. His family are entirely dependent upon him for support and the allotment received by the family is insufficient for their support.

This is a meritorious case and I would appreciate it very much if you would give the matter careful consideration.

Please let me know when a decision has been arrived at in the case.

Sincerely yours,

C. F. Curry.

Honorable Discharge with a fifteen per cent disability due to *pes planas.* So that's where I got my flat feet!

The stress of their daughter's disgrace, a son's hospitalization for shell shock, and complications of menopause led to the break-up of my grandparents' marriage. Grandmother remained in Oakland, and grandfather moved to Stockton.

When my mother married Albert Taylor, a barber, she "repossessed" Gene but left me with Grandmother, which brings us back to where we started.

CHAPTER 17

*"Some are born great, others achieve greatness,
others have greatness thrust upon them."*

Twelfth Night, Act II, Scene III.
William Shakespeare

My surrogate family tree also was rooted in the British Isles. Dad's great grandfather, David Madison Wood, was born in England in 1759 and emigrated to America with his father and two brothers. Initially, David settled in the "Half Moon" District, Saratoga County, New York, and married Mrs. Freelove Johnson, nee Thurston, of Eastontown, Albany County, on April 8, 1784. About 1790, the family moved to Augusta (near Knoxboro), Oneida County, New York. To this union twelve children were born (see chart -p. 267).[120]

William Wood was the tenth child and Dad's grandfather. He married Mahala Johnson, adopted daughter of Greelors Johnson and believed to be a full-blooded Iroquois Indian, an Oneida Mohawk. They had eleven children.

Cordelia "Dee" Wood married Captain George A.W. Bone. They had no issue, but she reared her nephews, David and John, Jr., following the death of their father John.

John G. Wood married Harriet Britton in 1855 and enlisted February 13, 1864, in Company A, 36th Wisconsin Volunteer Infantry, 1st Brigade, 2nd Division, 2nd Army Corps, Army of the Potomac. He died two months later of typhoid.

Marian Wood married Warren Brooks and had a daughter, Laura, and later married Antoine Rollette and had another girl, Eliza.

Amanda Maria Wood married Edward John Long, who emigrated from Ireland to America during the potato famine in 1846-47. He joined the 36th Regiment of the Northern Army during the Civil War and was

Back row:
Adelle A. Wood (Sp. Wm. Norton),
Cornelia E. Wood (Sp. G.W. Maddox, Sp. Thomas O'Brien).

Front row:
Amanda M. Wood (Sp. Edward John Long),
Cordelia Wood (Sp. George A.W. Bone), Marian Wood (Sp. Warren Brooks).

wounded at Lookout Mountain in 1864 and carried two Rebel bullets in his spine to his grave. After the war, he taught school and was ordained a minister of the Episcopalian Church. Born in County Tipperary, Ireland, in 1827, John called "Forte Edward" home, the Long Family Castle, which was located in the village of Ardmayle, a few miles north of Cashel. To make a long (no pun intended) story short, Dale M. Caragata, great, great grandson of Amanda Wood Long, traced the Long's ancestry back to the Royal House of Plantagenet, the Emperor Charlemagne, King John who signed the Magna Carta, King William the Conqueror (1066), King Alfred the Great, and King Cerdic (Cedric?) who died in 534 A.D. One ancestor, Katherine Roet, was sister-in-law to Geoffrey Chaucer. For the Royal Connection, please see *The Longs of Longfield* by Dale M. Caragata.

The fifth child, a daughter, died young.

George M. Wood, Dad's father, married Lorinda Faust, daughter of Abram Faust and Almira Aldridge (Aldrich), a direct descendant of Pocahontas, which made Dad one of the estimated two million descendants of the Powhatan princess. Another descendant, Edith Bolling Galt, of

Washington, D.C., became President Woodrow Wilson's second wife, December 18, 1915.

Elliot William Wood died at the age of twenty, unmarried.

Cornelia E. Wood was described by Theodore Roosevelt as "the best buckskin-maker I ever met . . . She made first-class hunting shirts, leggings, and gauntlets . . . She not only possessed redoubtable qualities of head and hand, but also a nice sense of justice, even toward Indians . . . I told her I sincerely wished we could make her sheriff and Indian Agent."[121] In his *Autobiography*, Roosevelt said "her husband [G.W. Maddux] was a worthless devil who . . . under the stimulus of . . . whiskey . . . attempted to beat her. She knocked him down with a stove-lid lifter . . . and told the admiring bull-whackers to [take him away], leaving the lady in full possession of the ranch. [The buckskin suit] she made for me and which I used for years, was used by one of my sons in Arizona a couple winters ago."[122]

Aunt Neal was also a woman who knew how to deal with drunken bullies. Too bad that pioneer spirit has died out. Later she married Thomas O'Brien.

Adelle Amelia Wood married William Norton and had eight children.

Theodore Roosevelt.
(Courtesy Dictionary of American Portraits)

Pocahontas.
(Courtesy Dictionary of American Portraits)

Back row:
George M. Wood (b. 1840-1, d. July 14, 1892),
Frank E. Wood (b. Dec. 6, 1866, d. June 25, 1958),
Lorinda Faust Wood (b. 1846, d. ca. 1900).

Front row:
Otha Charles Wood (b. June 10, 1871, d. Aug. 24, 1947),
Calvin Arthur Wood (b. May 20, 1867, d. Dec. 3, 1957).

Elnora Wood married Lester Hatch and had three daughters, Elizabeth, Laura, and Leona.

Last, but not least, was Charles A. Wood, born 1851, who was considered the "black sheep" of the family. However, there seems to be no records to substantiate this view.

Mother's branch of the surrogate family tree, the Flaughers, is not well documented. The earliest reference that I could find was Adam Flaugher, born in 1756 in Pennsylvania and died shortly after the Revolutionary War, in which he achieved the rank of Sergeant. He married —— Hidler, also of Pennsylvania.[123] Probably he was the grandfather of John M. Flaugher, born 1844, who married Rachel Anna Crowser April 28, 1868, in Story County, Iowa. Rachel A. Crowser was born October 28, 1846, to William Crowser, farmer, and Ruth Ballard Crowser. William was born in Virginia and wife, Ruth, in Ohio.

According to the 1850 Census records, William Crowser had an older brother, Moses, and two younger brothers, Lewis, born 1836, and Orren, born 1839, who married Isabel Mecum, February 28, 1865.

Rachel's siblings Caroline, Moses, James, and Martha were born in Illinois. Only Rachel was born in Iowa.

Rachel's brother, Moses, married Caroline (Catherine) Ballard July 8, 1869. The Cambridge Cemetery records show that Moses died June 1, 1883, and his wife, Catherine, died November 8, 1911.[124]

In 1870, Rachel Flaugher and one-year-old son, William, were living with her parents. Her second son, James, arrived the following year. According to my foster mother, Rachel then had three daughters. However, I have been unable to trace one of them. Martha "Mattie" Flaugher, born 9-14-1878, married O. C. Wood April 27, 1896. Almira (Almeda?) Flaugher, born July, 1875, married Aivy A. Rogers and had a son, Earl, born 1898-9.[125]

Half-brother, James Flaugher, married Elizabeth Pierce and had four children, two boys and two girls. Johnnie and Ralph died young, one of appendicitis and the other of pneumonia, in South Dakota. Bertha and Garnet came west with their parents to settle in Nevada. Bertha married Oscar Steward and had a son, Robert, and a daughter, Charlotte. Garnet wed Forrest Parry and had two boys, Lloyd and Gordon Parry. Lloyd was later murdered in San Francisco and Gordon served the city of Reno, Nevada, for thirty-six years as civil engineer.

Rachel's older son, William, participated in the Lincoln County Range War in New Mexico, and later he and his mother homesteaded one hundred fifty-nine and 23/100 acres at the north end of Long Valley, Washoe County, Nevada, in 1914.[126] When he died, his death was ruled an accident by gunshot.

Thus ends this branch of the Flaugher tree for lack of male issue to perpetuate the name.

CHAPTER 18

"The time is out of joint: O cursed spite,
That ever I was born to set it right!"

Hamlet, Prince of Denmark, Act I, Scene V.
William Shakespeare

If Shakespeare thought that "time was out of joint" in the sixteen hundreds, he should see us now.

How often we quote his "a rose by any other name would smell as sweet" but glibly parrot the latest "politically correct" new-speak, as if changing the label on a package altered its contents.

And poor Diogenes, who preached the doctrine of self-control and that morality implies a return to nature and simplicity, would need more than a lantern to find some common sense, let alone the truth today. Emotion is being substituted for the three R's of Reason, Responsibility, and Reality. Unfortunately, the emotional response to negative stimuli is violence.

Even the Constitution is not immune to the sophistry of the sentimentalists who spout the lines from Emma Lazarus' poem on the Statue of Liberty as government policy on immigration. In fact, the Immigration and Naturalization Service specifically excludes the indigent, the severely impaired, communicably diseased, felons, subversives, etc.

Another frequently misused argument in the name of equal opportunity comes from the Declaration of Independence: that all men are endowed equal, but they are *not* equally endowed. For instance, the five-foot man and the seven-foot man are not going to receive equal consideration for a position as a basketball center; the three hundred pound applicant will not have an even chance with a hundred pounder for a job as a jockey; a tin ear will not qualify one for a place in the Philharmonic orchestra, but might be an advantage in the pop music racket. This diversity of ability extends to all levels of competence. Anyone can learn to operate a computer (if motivated), but the person who can think as well will have an edge on the non-thinker.

Last but not least is the misinterpretation of our unalienable rights: life, liberty, and the pursuit of happiness. People do not seem to understand the difference between pleasure and happiness. Pleasure is defined as the fleeting gratification of the senses. Happiness is the enduring sense of well-being derived from accomplishment, achievement, a job well done—the product of one's own efforts.

The problems in education are man-made like most of our problems, but knowing the etiology of a problem is not a solution. Dad's philosophy on educating children was "teach them all you can *before* they are twelve and then put them on trust." Childhood ends at puberty. Once "the sap starts to run" (hormones), cognitive learning flies out the window. Consistent with this philosophy is Herman Epstein's "Brain Growth Periodization, based on experimental scientific fact." While Epstein says that the 12-14 year old learning plateau lasts only two years, I believe adolescence lasts much longer. "The social and emotional trauma of transescence today are vividly reflected in the tragic increases in the incidence of suicide, . . . addictive syndromes, and emotional illness,"[127] not to mention the proliferation of gang violence, drug use, and "adult" crime.

Today, rites of passage are associated with primitive cultures, but at least they were in sync with nature, as today's legal definition of childhood is not. Since the labor laws disenfranchised American youth from acquiring practical work experience, a new classification needs to be added to the social infrastructure that recognizes the changed status of adolescents, the period of life between puberty and maturity. Schools should adapt their curriculum to accommodate these maturational changes with more emphasis on vocational training, apprenticeships, part-time jobs, and community service. Or better yet establish federally subsidized Junior High Prep Schools for ages 12 to 16, similar to the English preparatory schools which serve the 7-14 age groups. These Prep Schools would be self-contained, gender segregated, holistic training centers located in remote areas like abandoned military bases, an economically sound recycling of existing facilities readily adaptable to educational purposes.

Since most people agree that health is a desirable goal, physical education at the Prep Schools would be directed toward lifelong health, not just the exploitation of a few star-quality athletes and cheerleaders. A regular regimen of calisthenics or aerobics is within the scope of all students and a good habit to develop. In most schools, the under-sized, over-sized, shy, awkward, and anti-social are allowed to fall through the cracks in physical training. Yet these are the ones who most need the benefits of regular exercise.

By providing a gun, drug, and pollution free environment, Prep Schools can provide a constructive alternative for the potential gang member, druggie, couch potato, and "wage orphans," whose parents are too busy earning a living to provide parenting.

The curriculum should include a course in "Problem solving without guns," a much needed subject that does not seem to be taught anywhere. The curriculum should also include practical things like cooking, cleaning, first aid, budgeting, nutrition, gardening, motor repair, woodwork, nature study, manners, etc. The television should be replaced with live entertainment, concerts, plays, variety shows, art exhibits, debates, etc., produced by the students themselves.

In their final year, they should be given extensive Driver Ed. practice so that they are experienced, therefore safer, drivers when they hit the public highways.

Remember the old saw, "All work and no play make Jack a dull boy"? Well, all play and no work make Jack, and Jill, juvenile delinquents.

Another example of emotion being substituted for fact is the subject of slavery. If we accept the fact that *Homo Zinjanthropus*, discovered by British anthropologist, Louis B. Leakey, in the Olduvai Gorge, Tanzania, in 1959, was the earliest human fossil, over 1,500,000 years old, then we must recognize that slavery also started in Africa. Probably the first slaves were prisoners of tribal wars or hostages. We know that slavery was common in Biblical times. The Pharoahs did not build those pyramids, slaves did. Historically, practically every culture has passed through a "slave" phase, but only in America have the sins of the fathers been visited on their sons in perpetuity, to compensate and provide preferential consideration for descendants of slaves.

We also shanghaied Chinese to this country as slave-labor to build the railroad, but when the Chinese were freed of the yoke of oppression, they became leaders in commerce and education, and the Japanese did likewise when they were released from internment centers after World War II. Seldom, if ever, are Chinese or Japanese found in prison or on welfare, and yet they had the same handicaps (different skin color, language barriers, and minority status) that are commonly used as excuses for failure in our society today. Maybe the real problem is attitude.

Another dirty word is *prejudice*. Heavens to Betsy! All God's "chillun" got prejudice, but only white Americans are supposed to change their cotton-pickin' ways. Now, I call that discrimination. I have many prejudices—whiskers, pointy-toed cowboy boots, and tattoos at the top of the list. I always wonder about a man with whiskers. Is he so insecure psychologically that he has to prove his masculinity by growing a beard, or is he trying to hide a major defect (like "The Minister's Black Veil" by Hawthorne), or is he just too lazy to shave? As some wit remarked about George Bernard Shaw, "A man can't help his relatives, but he can do something about his whiskers."

Cowboy boots are an affectation borrowed from south of the border by drug-store cowboys. Old time stockmen wore shoes so that they could still walk if their horse fell and broke a leg. In cowboy boots, a rider afoot is as helpless as a beached whale, which seems to confirm the Old West definition of a cowboy: a sheepherder with his brains knocked out or a hobo too lazy to walk.

To me, tattoos represent mutilation of the flesh and a suspect psyche.

Besides feeling guilty about the practice of slavery a hundred and thirty years ago (notice I did not say thirteen *decades* as the newscasters would have), we love to flagellate ourselves about introducing alcohol and venereal diseases to the native Americans, carefully ignoring the fact that *they* introduced us to tobacco, which is still killing thousands of people annually. At least the Indians had sense enough to restrict the use of tobacco to ceremonial occasions like the signing of peace treaties.

Of course, when we are not blaming ourselves for everything (talk about arrogance), we can blame any meteorological phenomena on El Niño. However, I always try to look on the bright side. The mud slingers were getting low on mud before El Niño delivered a new supply.

Although I would be the first to condemn pollution of the environment, I do not give man credit for global warming. Based on my understanding of meteorological principles, I believe that global warming is the natural precursor of the next ice age.

Actually I miss the good old days when we were all Americans, by birth or naturalization, before the hyphenated Americans took over. But if you can't lick 'em, join 'em. So henceforth, I *demand* to be labeled a *female American*, not to be confused with male Americans, native Americans, ugly

Americans, un-Americans, Canadian Americans, Mexican Americans, North Americans, Middle Americans, South Americans, minority Americans, Hmong Americans, Thai Americans, *ad nauseam*.

In the good old days, women knew that men did not invite them to hotel rooms to play tiddly-winks. If a woman chose to accept the invitation, she may have felt confident of her ability to control any situation that developed, or she may have had her own agenda, but, in all honesty, she could not plead ignorance or innocence.

I am still trying to figure out what special job skills can only be demonstrated or evaluated in the privacy of a hotel room.

For anyone who hasn't figured out the three thumps that Kato Kalen heard, it was the dog returning home with a bloody glove as a treasure trove. Without a key to the gate, the dog jumped over the fence and bumped the air conditioner which vibrated in recoil. The impact caused the dog to drop the glove and to forget it. Simple, when you think about it.

Speaking of gloves, quality gloves, designed for winter wear, do not shrink when they get wet. Why didn't the police check out the other 199 owners of the brand name shoes? If they could have been eliminated, their case would have been much stronger.

And if sloppy parallel parking were evidence of murder, the prisons would be full of "serial killers."

One factor which was not brought out during the presentation of forensic evidence was the difference in the "age" of the blood samples. It was obvious in the first television newscast photos that the blood spots on the cement walk were duller and darker (and therefore older) than the shinier, fresher blood stains at the crime scene. Like paint, blood reflects less light as it dries. If forensic science could "date" blood stains to the minute, witnesses and howling dogs would be redundant.

In the wrongful death suit brought by the family of the victims in which they reiterated that it was "the principle, not the money" that they cared about, many of us hyphenated Americans were surprised that the family did not donate their settlement to a non-profit organization for battered women. Or something.

Another example of emotion costing American taxpayers millions of dollars was the call "to save the Wild horses." In the first place, the "only truly wild horse remaining in the twentieth century is the so-called *equus przewalskii* discovered in western Mongolia in 1879—a small (12 hands), rough, uncouth pony that was pronounced of wholly feral ancestry and habits."[128]

The indigenous wild horses of North America were fossils long before Columbus discovered America.

The "wild horses" that the taxpayers were asked "to save" were common barnyard "hay burners" that were turned loose on public grazing land because they ate too much. Their owners couldn't afford to feed them. Without herd management, the horses soon came in conflict with the stockmen who leased grazing rights. Instead of taking a leaf from the history books and organizing annual regional round-ups of the horses, culling out the old and diseased animals, gelding the colts, staging a rodeo to defray costs, and then releasing the herds back to the wilds, they saddled the taxpayers with a new government program. In a few years, the old-fashioned method of culling, gelding the colts, and natural attrition would have stabilized the wild horse population at acceptable levels and provided rodeo entertainment at the same time.

Speaking of gelding, there is historic precedence for its use on *Homo sapiens.* "From remote antiquity among the Orientals and later Greece, eunuchs were employed to protect the Muslim harems and Egyptian royal blood lines." Contrary to popular belief, eunuchs are not deficient in "courage and intellectual vigor." Herodotus states that in Persia, they were prized for their fidelity.

In eighteenth century Italy, boys were castrated before puberty to prevent their soprano or contralto voices from changing. This practice ended with the Accession of Pope Leo XIII.

Voluntary eunuchs to avoid sexual sin or temptation appeared in early Christian ages, its votaries acting on the texts Matthew XIX 12, v. 28-30. In the third century, there was a sect of eunuchs, the Valesii, who castrated themselves and their guests, thinking thereby to serve God (Augustine). A similar sect in Russia is called Skopzi.[129]

To cut to the chase, my contention is that if gelding were justified on such frivolous grounds in the past, it is certainly justified today to control sex criminals, especially pedophiles. It is effective and economical, eliminating the need for incarceration or monitoring.

Well, common sense tells me that the time has come to sign off and to thank all my readers. May your lives be as rich and rewarding as mine.

ENDNOTES

1. Oregon State Board of Health, Division of Vital Statistics, Certified Copy of Birth Record, May 21, 1935.
2. National Personnel Records Center, Military Personnel Records, Certification of Military Service, March 7, 1996.
3. California State Board of Health, Division of Vital Statistics, Standard Certificate of Death, Certified Copy, April 11, 1995.
4. *Enterprise Record*, March 21, 1924, #69.
5. *Modoc County Record*, Vol. 100, No. 1, June 6, 1992, p. 3.
6. United States Postal Service, Record of Appointment of Postmasters, 1789-1932.
7. Dale M. Caragata, Genealogical charts.
8. *Ibid.*
9. Stuart E. Brown, *Pocahontas' Descendants*, revised edition of Wyndham Robertson's book *Pocahontas and Her Descendants*, (1887) Genealogical Publishing Co. 1994.
10. *Nevada State Journal*, April 18, 1927, p. 6.
11. *Ibid.*, August 22, 1924, p. 8.
12. *Ibid.*, September 9, 1924, p. 8.
13. *Ibid.*, August 27, 1924, p. 5.
14. *Ibid.*, July 15, 1924, p. 8.
15. *Ibid.*, July 22, 1924, p. 8.
16. *Ibid.*, April 18, 1927, p. 6.
17. Irving Stone, *Clarence Darrow for the Defense*, (New York, 1941), p. 390.
18. *Ibid.*, p. 391.
19. *Ibid.*, pp. 400-01.
20. *Ibid.*, p. 405.
21. *Nevada State Journal*, Washoe County Registered Voters, September 22, 1925, p. 8.
22. Nevada State Board of Health, Bureau of Vital Statistics, Duplicate Certificate of Death, December 6, 1995.
23. *Ibid.*
24. *Nevada State Journal*, July 9, 1924.
25. *Ibid.*, August 22, 1924, p. 8.

26. *Ibid.*, July 15, 1924, p. 8.

27. *Ibid.*, September 9, 1924, p. 8.

28. *Ibid.*

29. *National Geographic Magazine*, Vol. 20, Jan.-Dec., 1909, pp. 479-485. Abstract from "The Nevada Mouse Plague of 1907-08" by Stanley Piper, Farmers' Bulletin 352 USDA.

30. United States Postal Service, Record of Appointment of Postmasters, October 1789-1932.

31. *Alturas Plaindealer*, January 16, 1925, Vol. XXX, #11.

32. *Nevada State Journal*, September 27, 1925, p. 5.

33. *Modoc County Record*, August 7, 1997, p. 14.

34. State of California, County of Modoc, Certified copy of Vital Records, May 6, 1997.

35. *Ibid.*, May 20, 1997.

36. *Ibid*

37. Modoc County Record, Case No. 2675, 1925.

38. *Nevada State Journal*, July 26, 1925, p. 6.

39. State of California, County of Modoc, Certification of Vital Record, May 6, 1997.

40. *Alturas Plaindealer*, XXXI, July 9, 1926, p. 1.

41. *Ibid.*, July 16, 1926, p. 1.

42. Modoc County Court Records, Case No. 2844, People *vs* F.E. Page.

43. *Alturas Plaindealer*, July 9, 1926, p. 1.

44. *Nevada State Journal*, July 14, 1926, p. 2.

45. *Alturas Plaindealer*, XXXI, August 13, 1926, p. 1.

46. Edward F. Treadwell, *The Cattle King: A Dramatized Biography*, (New York, 1931), p. 5.

47. *Ibid.*, pp. 8-9.

48. *Ibid.*, pp. 17-18.

49. *Ibid.*, pp. 24-25.

50. *Ibid.*, Foreword, pp. vii-viii.

51. *Ibid.*, p. 187.

52. *Ibid.*, p. 334.

53. Fred S. Cook, *History of Modoc County*, California Traveler, Inc., 1954, p. 38.

54. *Northern California Traveler*, November 1993, pp. 4, 10.

55. *Alturas Plaindealer*, November 12, 1926, p. 1.

56. John Hay, "Miles Keogh's Horse, Comanche," Brown & Barron, pp. 57-9.

57. *Sturgis Weekly Record*, "The Double Tragedy," July 1892.

58. Assessment Rolls, 1920, Vol. 1, Modoc County, California.

59. Modoc County Records, Case No. 2844, May 24, 1927.

60. Hank Greene, *Square and Folk Dancing, (1984), p. 12.*

61. *Surprise Valley Record*, March 13, 1929.

62. *Ibid.*, January 28, 1931.

63. *Ibid.*, June 14, 1933.

64. *Ibid.*, June 13, 1932.

65. *Ibid.*, September 23, 1931.

66. *Ibid.*, July 15, 1931.

67. *Ibid.*, September 23, 1931.

68. *Ibid.*, July 20, 1931.

69. Cemetery Records, Cedarville, California.

70. *Surprise Valley Record*, November 25, 1931.

71. *Alturas New Era*, May 17, 1918.

72. *Surprise Valley Record*, January 9, 1929.

73. *Ibid.*, October 18, 1933.

74. United States Department of Interior - Fish and Wildlife Service. Sheldon - Hart Mountain Refuges.

75. *Works of Theodore Roosevelt, The*, Vol. I, Theodore Roosevelt. Introduction by - George Bird Grinnell, p. xvii. Charles Scribner's Sons, 1926, New York.

76. *Surprise Valley Record*, April 17, 1935.

77. *Ibid.*, May 15, 1935.

78. *Ibid.* November 27, 1935.

79. *Ibid.*, October 2, 1935.

80. *Alturas Plaindealer, The.* A Historical, Biographical, and Pictorial Magazine devoted to Modoc County, compiled by R.A. French, 1912, p. 34.

81. *Surprise Valley Record*, December 18, 1935.

82. *Ibid.* July 2, 1936.

83. *Ibid.*, August 27, 1936.

84. *Alturas Plaindealer*, January 18, 1939.

85. *Ibid.*, October 5, 1939.

86. *Sacramento Bee*, A 2, June 12, 1997, p. 2.

87. *Alturas Plaindealer*, July 25, 1940.

88. *Ibid.*, September 19 and November 7, 1940.

89. *Plaindealer Times*, June 1, 1944.

90. *Sacramento Bee*, July 7, 1996, Vol. 279, pp. A1, A18. "Recalling a Dark Moment," by Stephen Magagnini.

91. *Modoc County Record*, October 4, 1945.

92. *Modoc County Times*, October 25, 1928.

93. *Ibid.*, April 21, 1932.

94. *Surprise Valley Record*, September 7, 1932.

95. *Ibid.*, February 10, 1932.

96. *Modoc County Record*, July 18, 1946.

97. Modoc County Chamber of Commerce, Modoc Travel Loops, pp. 4, 20.

98. *American Armoury and Blue Book*, Vol. 2, p. 103. Mathews, London, 1908.

99. Jack Heald, President Heald Genealogical Society, submitted by E.P. Heald, La Mesa, California, 1969.

100. *Johnson's Wonder-Working Providence*, 1628-1651. Editor Franklin Jameson, Chapter XXXVI, pp. 111-112. Barnes and Noble, New York, 1910.

101. *Ibid.*, p. 7.

102. *Narratives of the Insurrections*, E. Charles M. Andrews, p. 182, New York, 1915.

103. *Ibid.*, p. 171.

104. Ancestral File, Descendancy Chart, John Heald, July 1996, Church of Jesus Christ of Latter Day Saints.

105. *DAR Patriot Index*, p. 318, Washington, D.C., 1966, Mrs. William Henry Sullivan, Jr., President-General.

106. Jack Heald, Letter, April 1, 1996.

107. *The People's Almanac*, David Wallechinsky and Irving Wallace, pp. 1267-68. Doubleday & Company, New York, 1975.

108. United States Census, Oxford County, Maine, 1860.

109. *San Francisco Chronicle*, July 12, 1925, p. 5.

110. *The History of the Comstock Lode*, 1850-1920, Nevada Bureau of Mines, p. 16. University of Nevada, 1966, by Grant Smith. Bulletin No. 3, Vol. XXXVII, July 1, 1943.

111. *The Saga of the Comstock Lode - Boom Days in Virginia City*, George D. Lyman, p. 126. Charles Scribner Sons, New York, 1941.

112. *Ibid.*, pp. 212-13.

113. *Ibid.*, p. 130.

114. *History of the Comstock Lode*, 1850-1920, Nevada Bureau of Mines, pp. 80, 84. University of Nevada, 1966, by Grant Smith, Bulletin No. 3, Vol. XXXVII, July 1, 1943.

115. *Ibid.*, pp. 238-240.

116. *Richest Place on Earth*, Warren Hinkle and Frederic Hobbs, p.36. Houghton Mifflin Company, Boston, 1978.

117. *Ibid.*, pp. 132-3.

118. United States Census, 1880, San Francisco, Ward 12.

119. Letter, Representative C.F. Curry to Major-General George Barnett, September 20, 1919.

120. Genealogical Charts, Wood Family, Dale M. Caragata, 1984.

121. *The Works of Theodore Roosevelt*, Vol. 1, Theodore Roosevelt, p. 368. Charles Scribner & Sons, New York, 1926.

122. *Theodore Roosevelt: An Autobiography*. Theodore Roosevelt, pp. 110-11.

123. *DAR Patriot Index*, p.240, Washington, D.C., 1966. Mrs. William Henry Sullivan, Jr., President-General.
124. Assorted Genealogical Records of Story County, Iowa, Section 3, Marriage Records compiled by E.L. DeKalb. Iowa Genealogical Society, Des Moines, Iowa.
125. United States Census, 1900, Pennington County, South Dakota.
126. Land Patent Records, Reno, Nevada, Book C, p.137.
127. *Middle School Journal*, Conrad F. Toepper, Jr., August 1979, Vol. X, No. 3, pp. 18-20.
128. *Encyclopedia Britannica*, Vol. 11, pp. 754-57.
129. *Ibid.*, Vol. 8, p. 814.

BIBLIOGRAPHY

American Armoury and Blue Book, Vol. 2, Editor Mathews, London: 1908.

Andrews, Charles M., Editor, *Narratives of the Insurrections, 1675-1690*. Barnes & Noble, New York: 1943.

Brown, Stuart E., *Pocahontas' Descendants*, revised edition of Wyndham Robertson's book *Pocahontas and her Descendants*, (1887), Genealogical Publishing Company, 1994.

Cook, Fred S., *History of Modoc County*, California Traveler, Inc., 1954.

DAR Patriot Index, National Society of the Daughters of the American revolution. Mrs. William Henry Sullivan, Jr., *President-General*. Washington, D.C.: 1966.

Greene, Hank, *Square and Folk Dancing*, Harper & Row, New York: 1984.

Hay, John, *Comanche*, "Miles Keogh's Horse," Brown & Barron, New York: Sol Lewis, 1973.

Hinkle, Warren and Frederic Hobbs, *Richest Place on Earth*, Houghton Mifflin Company, Boston: 1978.

Jameson, Franklin, Editor. *Johnson's Wonder-Working Providence*, Barnes & Noble, New York: 1910.

Lyman, George D., *Saga of the Comstock Lode -Boom Days in Virginia City*, Charles Scribner Sons, New York: 1941.

Roosevelt, Theodore, *Theodore Roosevelt: An Autobiography*, Scribner, New York, 1920.

Roosevelt, Theodore, *The Works of Theodore Roosevelt*, Vol. 1, Introduction by George Bird Grinnell. Charles Scribner's Sons, New York: 1926.

Smith, Grant, *History of the Comstock Lode*, 1850-1920, Nevada Bureau of Mines, University of Nevada, 1966.

Stone, Irving, *Clarence Darrow for the Defense*, Doubleday, New York: 1941.

Treadwell, Edward F., *The Cattle King: A Dramatized Biography*, Macmillan Company, New York: 1931.

Wallechinsky, David and Irving Wallace, Editors, *The People's Almanac*, Doubleday & Company, New York: 1975.

PERIODICALS

Alturas New Era, May 17, 1918.

Alturas Plaindealer, XXX, (January 16, 1925), XXXI (July 9, 1926), 1; (July 16, 1926) p. 1; (August 13, 1926) p. 1; (November 12, 1926) p. 1; (January 18, 1939); (October 5, 1939); (July 25, 1940); (September 19, 1940); (November 7, 1940).

Alturas Plaindealer, The, A Historical, Biographical, and Pictorial Magazine devoted to Modoc County, compiled by R.A. French, 1912.

Enterprise Record, March 21, 1924.

Modoc County Record, C (June 6, 1992), 3; (August 7, 1997), p. 14; (October 4, 1945); (July 18, 1946).

Modoc County Times, (October 25, 1928); (April 21, 1932).

Nevada State Journal, (April 18, 1927) p. 6; (August 22, 1924) p. 8; (September 9, 1924) p. 8; (August 27, 1924) p. 5; (July 15, 1924) p. 8; (July 22, 1924) p. 8; (September 22, 1925) p. 8; (July 9, 1924); (August 22, 1924) p. 8; (September 27, 1925) p. 5; (July 26, 1925) p. 6; (July 14, 1926) p. 2.

Northern California Traveler, (November 1993) pp. 4, 10.

Piper, Stanley, "The Nevada Mouse Plague of 1907-08," *National Geographic Magazine*, XX (Jan.-Dec., 1909), 479-485. U.S.D.A. Farmers' Bulletin 352.

Plaindealer Times, (June 1, 1944).

Sacramento Bee, A2, (June 12, 1997) p. 2.

San Francisco Chronicle, (July 12, 1925) p. 5.

Sturgis Weekly Record, "The Double Tragedy," (July 1892).

Surprise Valley Record, (March 13, 1929); (January 28, 1931); (June 14, 1933); (June 13, 1932); (September 23, 1931); (July 15, 1931); (July 20, 1931); (November 25, 1931); (January 9, 1929); (October 18, 1933); (April 17, 1935); (May 15, 1935); (November 27, 1935); (October 2, 1935); (December 18, 1935); (July 2, 1936); (August 27, 1936); (September 7, 1932); (February 10, 1932).

Toepper, Conrad F., Jr., "Brain Growth Periodization - A New Dogma for Education," *Middle School Journal*, X (August 1979), 18-20.

DOCUMENTS

Ancestral Files, Descendancy Chart, John Heald, 1996, Courtesy of Church of Jesus Christ of Latter Day Saints.

Assessment Rolls, 1920 Vol. 1. Modoc County, California.

Assorted Genealogical Records of Story County, Iowa, Section 3, Marriage Records compiled by E.L. DeKalb. Iowa Genealogical Society, Des Moines, Iowa.

California State Board of Health, Division of Vital Statistics, Standard Certificate of Death, Certified copy, April 11, 1995.

Caragata, Dale M., Genealogy Charts, Wood Family, 1984.

Cemetery Records, Cedarville, California.

Curry, C. F., Letter to Major-General George Barnett, September 20, 1919. National Personnel Records.

Heald, Jack, President Heald Genealogical Society. Copies of John and Samuel Heald documents. Copy of Will submitted by E.P. Heald, La Mesa, California, 1969. Letter, April 1, 1996.

Land Patent Records, Book C, p. 137, Reno, Nevada.

Modoc County Chamber of Commerce, Modoc Travel Loops, pp. 4, 20.

Modoc County Court Records, Case No. 2675, 1925. Case No. 2844, People *vs* F.E. Page, May 24, 1927.

National Personnel Records Center, Military Personnel Records, Certification of Military Service, March 7, 1996.

Nevada State Board of Health, Bureau of Vital Statistics, Duplicate Certificate of Death, December 6, 1995.

Oregon State Board of Health, Division of Vital Statistics, Certified Copy of Birth Record, May 21, 1935.

State of California, County of Modoc, Certified copies of Vital Records, May 6, 1997, and May 20, 1997.

United States Census, Oxford County, Maine, 1860.

United States Census, Pennington County, South Dakota, 1900.

United States Census, San Francisco County, California, 1880.

United States Department of Interior, Fish and Wildlife Service, Sheldon-Hart Mountain Refuges, January 6, 1995.

United States Postal Service, Record of Appointment of Postmasters, 1789-1932.

Encyclopedias

"Eunuch," *Encyclopedia Britannica*, Vol. 8, p. 814. Encyclopedia Britannica, Inc., 1956.

"Horse," *Encyclopedia Britannica*, Vol. 11, pp. 754-57. Encyclopedia Britannica, Inc., 1956.

EDWARDS FAMILY GENEALOGY CHART

1. Edwards, John b. 1825 d. 3-9-1897.
   Sp. Tyndall, Lucinda
   2. Edwards, Richard Joseph b. 1-16-1850. d. 6-22-1922.
      Sp. Graham, Eliza Ann b. 4-25-1857 d.3-23-1944.
      m. 7-3-1873.
      3. Edwards, John
         Sp. ———, Cora
      3. Edwards, Frank
         Sp. ———, Nora
         4. Edwards, Pearl
         4. Edwards, Dorothy
         4. Edwards, Marjorie
      3. Edwards, George Bentley b. 2-19-1881 d. 1-15-1940.
         Sp. Kessler, Mable Beatrice b. 1891 d. 1930
         4. Edwards, William Taft b. 12-13-1908 d. 1-15-1978.
            Sp. Godfrey, E. Maxine (Tendering) b. 11-1-1919.
            m. 9-23-1947.
            5. Edwards, Judith Ione b. 8-10-1949.
               6. Freeman, Josef Sergi b. 2-25-1970.
                  Sp. Barton, Evelyn m. 12-24-1988.
                  7. Freeman, Anthony Michael b. 8-19-1989.
                  7. Freeman, Brittany Marie b. 4-12-1991.
                  7. Freeman, Rook Alexander b. 12-30-1993.
               Sp. Goodwin, John m. 4-1971.
               6. Goodwin, Gabriel Gibran b. 5-10-1971
                  Sp. Erickson, Tammy Lee m. 12-16-89.
               6. Goodwin, Benjamin Xavier b. 10-14-72
                  d. 10-10-94.
               6. Goodwin, Phaedra Ann b. 6-4-1975
                  Sp. Mort, Kenneth Lloyd m. 7-15-1993.
                  7. Mort, Damaris Constantine b. 6-17-1993.
                  7. Mort, Dominique Chantilly b. 11-15-1997.
               6. Goodwin, Amber Joan b. 3-7-1978.
               6. Lopez, Chelsea Kim b. 5-3-1982.

5. Edwards, Audrey Carol b. 6-10-1951
   Sp. Chittenden, Robert, Jr.
     6. Chittenden, Elizabeth Zay b. 7-18-1972.
       7. White, Zach b. 6-28-1988.
     Sp. Satterwhite, Bryan
       7. Satterwhite, Tyler Lindsay b. 11-11-1992.
       7. Satterwhite, Seth Robert b. 9-18-1995.
       7. (Chittenden), Caleb b. 3-13-1998.
5. Edwards, Thomas Allan b. 9-15-1952.
4. Edwards, Irene B. b. 6-29-1911 d. 4-8-90.
  Sp. Dorris, ———-
  5. Dorris, Marvin
  Sp. Allin, Ronnie
4. Edwards, Evalyn
  Sp. Bauman, Chris
  5. Bauman, Althea (Dolly)
    Sp.
     6.
     6.
  5. Bauman, Buzzy
  5. Bauman, Clay
4. Edwards, Kenneth Karl b. 6-3-1916 d. 11-23-89.
  Sp. Pettigrew, Mavis Ethel
  5. Pettigrew, Ray Phillip b. 1-5-1938.
  5. Edwards, Sylvia Jean b. 12-19-1941.
  5. Edwards, Alan Keith b. 1-27-1943.
  5. Edwards, Sharon Lynn b. 2-27-1944.
  5. Edwards, Kathleen Karen b. 12-31-1946.
  5. Edwards, Norma Lou b. 3-10-1948.
  5. Edwards, Rodger Wayne b. 7-2-1949.
4. Edwards, Richard
  Sp. ———-, Lucille
4. Edwards, Allen Henry b. 2-21-1923
  Sp. Silvesan, Delmarine Della
  5. Edwards, Ralph Leon b. 1946.
  5. Edwards, Laura Grace b. 10-2-1951.
  5. Edwards, Bruce William b. 12-18-1952.
4. Edwards, Rodger b. 4-11-1925 d. 11-22-1977.
  Sp. ———-, Jackie
4. Edwards, Catherine Joan b. 2-4-1928
                   d. 8-23-1989.
  Sp. Kessler, Francis Charles d. 1983/4.

     5. Kessler, Tony b. 3-15-1951.
     5. Kessler, Ron b. 11-6-1954.
3. Edwards, Arthur Byron b. 3-15-1882 d. 1947.
   Sp. Babcock, Helen Louise b. 5-31-1881 d. 12-1-59.
     4. Edwards, Eudora b. 1906 d. 1909.
     4. Edwards, Lela Alice Mary b. 8-19-1909 d. 9-23-1955.
     Sp. Duggan, Sydney
     Sp. Beck, ———- m. 11-24-1926.
   Sp. ———-, May
     4. Edwards, Eugene Leo d. 1983.
3. Edwards, Acy Ray b. 1-16-1885 d. 4-18-1950.
   Sp. Rairden, Millie Emma b. 7-7-1886 d. 5-16-1968.
                            m. 1-2-1905.
     4. Edwards, Leslie R. b. 9-17-1905.
     4. Edwards, Dorothy b. 3-23-1907 d. 3-23-1907.
     4. Edwards, George Ivan b. 2-22-1908
     4. Edwards, Mona Estella b. 11-28-1909.
     4. Edwards, Milo Richard b. 9-27-1911 d. 12-17-91.
     4. Edwards, Florence Imogene b. 2-18-1914.
     4. Edwards, Robert Acy b. 5-21-1916 d. 5-22-1916.
     4. Edwards, Paul Quentin b. 8-15-1918 d. 3-27-1989.
     4. Edwards, John Lloyd b. 11-11-1920 d. 12-12-1920.
     4. Edwards, Klyda May b. 10-23-1921 d. 12-11-1974.
     4. Edwards, Lynn Frazer b. 7-18-1924
     4. Edwards, Shirley Jo b. 2-8-1927.
3. Edwards, Ella Winona b. 7-7-1887 d. 8-28-1917.
   Sp. Pfaff, Charles b. 6-4-1885 m. 3-8-1961.
     4. Pfaff, Theodore E. b. 6-1-1908 d. 2-22-1986.
     4. Pfaff, Lillian b. 5-27-1910.
3. Edwards, Emma b. 5-20-1890 d. 9-30-1975.
   Sp. Claymore, William S. b. 3-17-1881 d. 11-16-1961.
     4. Claymore, Grant William b. 4-27-1916 d. 4-18-1970.
     Sp. Bailey, Catherine Beatrice m. 10-4-1942.
     4. Claymore, Joseph James b. 4-9-1919 d. 8-25-1963.
     Sp. Graham, Katherine Elizabeth m. 12-9-1947.
     4. Claymore, Richard Clinton b. 5-6-1921 d. 3-29-1983.
     Sp. Riddle, June Wallace m. 6-1947.
     4. Claymore, Billy Stewart b. 6-30-1924.
3. Edwards, Joseph Richard b. 1-14-1893 d. 4-4-1941.
3. Edwards, Paul Irvin b. 4-27-1896 d. 11-1-1903

2. Edwards, Arthur Byron
2. Edwards, Henry
2. Edwards, Tom
2. Edwards, George (Ed Edwards) Bond. b. 1858.
2. Edwards, Emma

FLETCHER FAMILY DESCENDANCY CHART
(ABRIDGED)

---

1. Fletcher, William b. ca 1502 Cocker, Cumberland, England.
   Sp. Swinbarr, ——— b. ca 1502 Huthwait
   2. Fletcher, Lancelot b. ca 1530 Cockermouth Castle, Cumberland, England.
      Sp. Unknown
      3. Fletcher, William b. ca 1570 Cockermouth Castle, Cumberland, England
         Sp. Unknown
         4. Fletcher, Robert b. 1591-2 Skropshire, Yorkshire, England.
            Sp. Hailstone, Margaret b. 1592
            5. Fletcher, Grissell b. 1612-18 Chelmsford, Eng.
               Sp. Jewell, Thomas
            5. Fletcher, William b. 1619-22.
               Sp. Bates, Lydia b. 6-1622 Boston, Lancashire, England.
               6. Fletcher, John b. 1645
                  Sp. Heald, Dorothy b. 8-16-1649.
               6. Fletcher, Lydia b. 3-30-1646.
                  Sp. Fiske, John.
               6. Fletcher, Joshua b. 3-3-1648.
                  Sp. Jewell, Grissell.
                  7. Fletcher, Joshua, Jr. b. 1-4-1677.
                     Sp. Hale (Heald), Dorothy b. 7-10-1679.
                     8. Fletcher, Joshua b. 5-1-1701.
                        Sp. Blodgett, Elizabeth b. 12-15-1699.
                        9. Fletcher, Joshua b. 7-10-1724.
                        9. Fletcher, Esther b. 9-14-1726.
                     8. Fletcher, Gershom b. 7-27-1702.
                        Sp. Townsend, Lydia b. 1712.
                        9. Fletcher, Lydia b. 2-18-1733/4.
                           Sp. Prescott, Timothy
                           (11 children)
                        9. Fletcher, Esther b. 12-13-1735.
                           Sp. Tarbell, James b. 10-11-1725. (3 children)

9. Fletcher, Gershom, Jr. b. 9-30-1737.
   Sp. Robinson, Sarah b. 1741.
   10. Fletcher, Sarah b. 8-28-1770.
   10. Fletcher, Gershom, III b.11-22-1771.
   10. Fletcher, Jacob b. 3-12-1773.
   10. Fletcher, Lucy b. 3-6-1775.
   10. Fletcher, Stephen b. 10-22-1776.
   10. Fletcher, Dorothy b. 9-28-1778.
       Sp. Parker, Elias b. 1771.
   10. Fletcher, Gershom b. 9-30-1780.
9. Fletcher, Olive b. 8-14-1741.
9. Fletcher, Sarah b. 4-14-1744.
   Sp. Corey, Hezekiah b. 1740.
9. Fletcher, Mary b. 7-2-1746.
   Sp. Robbins, Jonathan
   b. 1744 d. 12-8-1819 (2 children).
9. Fletcher, Lucy b. 9-15-1751.
9. Fletcher, Martha b. 6-1754.
   Sp. Reed, Joseph (2 children).
9. Fletcher, Joshua b. 9-24-1756.
   Sp. Brown, Sarah.
   10. Fletcher, Joshua, Jr. 5-16-1776.
       Sp. Pulsifer, Sarah b. 1780.
   10. Fletcher, Joseph b. 1778.
       Sp. Webster, Betsy b. 5-1782.
   10. Fletcher, Gershom 8-28-1780.
       Sp. Hush, Elizabeth b. 1784.
   10. Fletcher, Nathan b. 1783.
       Sp. Pillsbury, Nancy b. 1787.
   10. Fletcher, Samuel b. 7-31-1785.
       Sp. Boardman, Nancy
   10. Fletcher, William Asa b. 6-26-1788 d.
       9-19-1852.
       Sp. Hamilton, Gertrude b. 1792.
   10. Fletcher, Amos b. 7-13-1790.
       Sp. Gale, Abigail b. 1794.
       Sp. Gould, Sally b. 1794.
   10. Fletcher, Sarah b. 1792.
   10. Fletcher, Daniel b. 1794.
8. Fletcher, Sarah b. 2-25-1703.
8. Fletcher, Elizabeth b. 2-9-1705.
   Sp. Blodgett, Benjamin b. 1704.
   Sp. Parker, ———— b. 1704.

8. Fletcher, Hannah b. 9-21-1706.
   Sp. Barron, Timothy b. 3-30-1707.
   (16 ? children)
8. Fletcher, Esther b. 10-29-1708.
8. Fletcher, Ephraim b. 3-12-1710.
   Sp. Roe, Hannah.
   9. Fletcher, Joshua b. 10-19-1734.
   9. Fletcher, Peter b. 1-22-1736.
      Sp. Adams, Ruth b. 1-3-1739.
      10. Fletcher, Dorothy b. 2-14-1763.
      10. Fletcher, Ruth b. 10-10-1765.
         Sp. Batchelder, ———— b. 1761
      10. Fletcher, Peter b. 1-8-1768.
         Sp. Taylor, Thirza 11-15-1778.
      10. Fletcher, Ebenezer 5-17-1770.
         Sp. Smith, Peday ? b. 1774.
      10. Fletcher, David b. 12-28-1772.
         Sp. Lovell, Sally b. 1776.
      10. Fletcher Submit b. 11-6-1774.
      10. Fletcher, James b. 7-1776.
      10. Fletcher, James b. 12-27-1778.
         Sp. Gale, Azuba b. 1782.
      10. Fletcher, Lydia b. 11-12-1781.
         Sp. Spencer, John.
   9. Fletcher, Lois b. 1-18-1741.
   9. Fletcher, Sarah b. 1-23-1742.
   9. Fletcher, Ephraim, Jr. b. 5-26-1743.
8. Fletcher, Zachariah b. 10-28-1714.
   Sp. Fasset, Susannah b. 1717.
   9. Fletcher, Zechariah b. 3-11-1735.
   9. Fletcher, Susannah b. 9-25-1737.
   9. Fletcher, Zechariah b. 6-23-1740.
      Sp. ————, Eunice b. 1744.
      10. Fletcher, Eunice b. 3-20-1763.
      10. Fletcher, Susannah 8-12-1765.
      10. Fletcher, Abigail 6-13-1768.
   9. Fletcher, Susannah b. 10-24-1743.
      Sp. Parker, Joseph b. 1739.
   9. Fletcher, Joshua b. 9-4-1745.
   9. Fletcher, Abigail b. 1747.
   9. Fletcher, Elizabeth b. 1749.
8. Fletcher, Dorothy b. 3-17-1714.?
   Sp. Parker, Aaron b. 8-19-1713.

8. Fletcher, Sarah b. 3-29-1719.
Sp. Parker, Samuel b. 1-1-1717.
8. Fletcher, Eunice b. 11-9-1720.
Sp. Fasset, Amiziah b. 1716.
5. Fletcher, Luke b. 1620/21 England.
5. Fletcher, Francis b. 5-10-1626.
(Grandfather Heald's namesake)
Sp. Wheeler, Elizabeth b. 1-3-1636.
6. Fletcher, Samuel b. 10-6-1657.
Sp. Hailston, Margaret
6. Fletcher, Joseph b. 4-15-1661.
Sp. Dudley, Mary b. 2-7-1666.
6. Fletcher, Elizabeth b. 8-24-1663.
Sp. Stratton, Samuel b. 3-5-1660.
6. Fletcher, John b. 2-28-1665.
Sp. Hunt, Hannah b. 6-5-1670.
6. Fletcher, Sarah b. 2-24-1668 (twin ?)
Sp. Wheeler, William b. 2-8-1665.
6. Fletcher, Samuel b. 1668 (twin ?)
6. Fletcher, Hezekiah b. 4-6-1672. d.1722.
Sp. Wood, Mary b. 6-25-1686
7. Fletcher, William b. 10-15-1710 d. 7-4-1760.
Sp. Heald, Dorcas
b. 8-22-1713
m. 1-28-1734/5.
8. Fletcher, William, Jr. b. 1736.
Sp. Wheeler, Sarah
8. Fletcher, Mary b. 9-16-1750.
Sp. Bond, Henry
6. Fletcher, Hannah b. 10-24-1674.
Sp. Wheeler, Obadiah
6. Fletcher, Benjamin b. 12-1-1677.
Fletcher, Rebeccah b. 11-13-1717
Sp. Heald, Samuel b. 5-4-1705.
Heald, Samuel, Jr. b. 3-27-1743 d. 5-11-1829.
Sp. Hunt, Mary
Fletcher, Esther b. 1744.
Sp. Heald, Oliver b. 8-1-1740.

* * * * * * * * * *

Other descendants of Robert Fletcher:

Fletcher, Jesse
Sp. Keyes, Lucy m. 8-8-1782.
    Fletcher, Calvin b. 2-4-1798 d. 5-26-1866.
    Sp. Hill, Sarah m. 5-1-1821.
        Fletcher, James Cooley b. 4-15-1823 d. 4-23-1901.
        Fletcher, William Baldwin b. 8-18-1837 d. 4-25-1907.
        Sp. Brown, Sarah
    Sp.(2) Mrs. Keziah Price Lister (Backhurst) m. 11-5-1855.

Fletcher, Asaph
Sp. Green, Sarah
    Fletcher, Richard b. 1-8-1788 d. 6-21-1869.

Fletcher, Grace m. Daniel Webster 1808.

Fletcher, Isaac
Sp. Blake, Mary
    Fletcher, Horace b. 8-10-1840 d. 1-13-1919.

GODFREY FAMILY GENEALOGY CHART

1. Godfrey, Elasher b. c 1820 d. c 1885 m. 6-15-1846.
   Sp. Martin, Elizabeth b. 4-18-1818/9 d. 1-3-1925.
   2. Godfrey, George b. 8-29-1847.
   2. Godfrey, Sarah b. 11-11-1849 d. 12-1935.
      Sp. Richer, Frank b. 8-3-1835 d. 3-1919.
   2. Godfrey, Abbie b. 5-30-1853 d. 1-18-1939.
   2. Godfrey, Charles F. b. 5-11-1856 d. 3-20-1941.
      Sp. Stanley, Minnie M.
          b. 8-18-1874 d. 10-10-1951.
          m. 5-18-1896.
      3. Godfrey, Mertie Elizabeth b. 3-9-1897 d. 1-21-1964.
         Sp. Link. Chester m. 12-23-1920.
         4. Link, Wilbur b. 7-2-1922.
            Sp. Thompson, Otis m. 5-24-1937.
      3. Godfrey, LeRoy E. b. 12-11-1898 m. 9-4-1937 d. 1982 ?
         Sp. Wood, E. Maxine (Tendering) b. 11-1-1919.
         4. Godfrey, Charles LeRoy b. 7-6-1938.
            Sp. Chaltron, Joan Ann m. 8-12-1960.
            5. Godfrey, Laurie Ann b. 8-27-1961
            5. Godfrey, Chuck, Jr. b. 10-26-1963.
               Sp. Whelchel, LaWanda Joetta (Beasly) b. 3-12-1945.
               (Whelchel, Rayetta Ray b. 6-27-1965.)
               (Whelchel, Danny Ray b. 9-18-1967)
            5. Godfrey, Deborah Lynn b. 4-16-1971.
               Sp. Forsee, Scott
               Sp. Fernandez, Toby m. 2-24-1995.
               6. Fernandez, Tanner S. b. 8-23-1995.
            5. Godfrey, Christina Marie b. 12-16-1972
               Sp. Bierdermann, Pete m. 5-6-1995.
            5. Godfrey, Patricia b. 1-27-1977.
            5. Godfrey, Patrick b. 1-27-1977.
               Sp. Bohmer, Christel m. 2-14-1995.

4. Godfrey, Stephen Adair b. 7-1-1939 m. 8-5-1961.
  Sp. Green, Ida May b. 9-18-1939.
  Sp. Boyd, Danny
  Sp. Claudell, William
  5. Claudell, Nell Ora b. 2-28-1961.
    Sp. Wattenburg, Jerry
    6. Wattenburg, Christopher Lee b. 4-19-1980.
    6. Wattenburg, Raymond Jennings b. 10-5-1981
    6. Wattenburg, Jerry, Jr. b. 10-27-1983 d. 1-1984
    6. Wattenburg, Jason Allan b. 6-28-1985
    6. Wattenburg, Bryan Clare b. 4-22-1988
  5. Godfrey, Lyndell May b. 5-7-1962
    Sp. Jaques, Billy
    Sp. Prosser, Tim m. 7-1-1989
    6. Prosser, Brittany Rayne b. 11-28-1989
    6. Prosser, Brent Stephen b. 8-6-1992
    6. Prosser, Brandon Michael b. 3-26-1994.
  5. Godfrey, Recy Ann b. 2-23-1965
    Sp. Scott, Troy
    6. Scott, NellOra Danielle b. 9-16-1985
      Sp. Ferris, Danny
  5. Godfrey, Lois Rae b. 3-5-1968
    Sp. Fackrell, Rex
    6. Fackrell, Steven b. 10-15-1993
    6. Fackrell, Cameron b. 10-1-1995
    6. Fackrell, Aaron b. 8-16-1997
3. Godfrey, Nellie M. b. 1-9-1902 d. 9-21-1995.
 Sp. Anderson, Martin m. 8-25-1924.
  4. Anderson, Richard Rollin b. 7-28-1926 d. 8-25-1975
  Sp. Steffen, Janet m. 7-2-1960.
    5. Anderson, Dale Martin b.3-25-1967.
    5. Anderson, Douglas Edward b. 2-2-1971.
  4. Anderson, LeRoy G. b. 9-16-1928 m. 7-6-1948.
  Sp. Bass, Darlene b. 6-26-1932.
    5. Anderson, Diana b. 7-10-1949.
    Sp. Watson, Perry m. 6-30-1970.
    6. Watson, David LeRoy b. 1-7-1972.
    6. Watson, Daniel Martin b. 10-15-1974
    5. Anderson, Tommie b. 9-13-1951. m. 6-27-1970.
    Sp. Standiford, Donnie b. 9-8-1953 d. 5-26-1974
    6. Anderson, Theresa b. 1-5-1971.
    5. Anderson, Jerry b. 12-6-1955.

3. Godfrey, Lillie L. b. 7-26-1907 m. 11-29-1929 d.
    Sp. Kafader, Louis b. 5-2-1882 d. 2-21-1954.
       4. Kafader, Louis Gene b. 8-31-1936 d.
          Sp. Quector ?, Dorothy Ann m. 9-1-1956.
             5. Kafader, Theresa May b. 7-24-1957.
                Sp. Westbrook, N.R. m. 7-14-1975.
             5. Kafader, Helen Louise b. 3-2-1961.
             5. Kafader, Neva Ralene b. 5-24-1965.
             5. Kafader, Christian Daniel b. 8-21-1974.
                Sp. Hatfield, Lewis C. b. 3-5-1895 d. 8-13-1963
                                    m. 7-1-1960.
3. Godfrey, Frank H. b. 8-14-1909 d. 10-15-1909.
3. Godfrey, Charley T. b. 5-10-1911 d. 10-5-1995.

MENDELL-STANLEY FAMILY DESCENDANCY CHART

1. Solomon Mendell b. 6-3-1825 PA d. 2-28-1902
   Sp. Nancy Gibson b. 9-6-1832 Ind. d. 1907 Ore.
   2. Rachel Elizabeth Mendell b. 4-25-1856 d.5-31-1923
      Sp. Harbor Stanley b. 9-16-1850 m. 11-9-1873 d. 8-25-1887
      3. Minnie May Stanley b. 8-18-1874 d. 10-10-1951
         Sp. Charles F. Godfrey b. 5-11-1856 d. 3-20-1941
                                           m. 5-18-1896
         4. Mertie Elizabeth Godfrey b. 3-9-1897 d. 1-21-1964
            Sp. Chester Link m. 12-23-1920
            5. Wilbur Link b. 7-2-1922
               Sp. Otis Thom(p)son m. 5-24-1937
         4. LeRoy E. Godfrey b. 12-11-1898 d.
            Sp. Elizabeth Maxine Wood (Tendering) b. 11-1-1919
                                           m. 9-4-1937
            5. Charles LeRoy Godfrey b. 7-6-1938
               Sp. Joan Ann Chaltron m. 8-12-1960
               6. Laurie Ann Godfrey b. 8-27-1961
               6. Chuck Godfrey, Jr. b. 10-26-1963
                  Sp. LaWanda Joetta Beasly Whelchel
                  Sp. Ray Whelchel (Rayetta Ray Whelchel b. 6-27-65)
                  (Danny Ray Whelchel b. 9-18-67)
               6. Deborah Lynn Godfrey b. 4-16-1971
                  Sp. Scott Forsee
                  Sp. Toby Fernandez m. 2-24-95
                  7. Tanner S. Fernandez b. 8-23-95
               6. Christina Marie Godfrey b. 12-16-72
                  Sp. Pete Biedermann m. 5-6-95
               6. Patrick Godfrey b. 1-27-77
               6. Patricia Godfrey b. 1-27-77
            5. Stephen Adair Godfrey b. 7-1-1939
               Sp. Ida May Green b. 9-18-1939
                  Sp. Danny Boyd
                  Sp. William Claudell

Nell Ora Claudell b. 2-28-1961
Sp. Jerry Wattenburg
    Christopher Lee Wattenburg b. 4-19-1980
    Raymond Jennings Wattenburg b. 10-5-1981
    Jerry Wattenburg, Jr. b. 10-27-1983 d. 1-1984
    Jason Allan Wattenburg b. 6-28-1985
    Bryan Clare Wattenburg b. 4-22-1988
6. Lyndell May Godfrey b. 5-7-1962
Sp. Billy Jaques
Sp. Tim Prosser m. 7-1-1989
    7. Brittany Rayne Prosser
          b. 11-28-1989
    7. Brent Stephen Prosser
          b. 8-6-1992
    7. Brandon Michael Prosser
          b. 3-26-1994
6. Recy Ann Godfrey b. 2-23-1965
Sp. Troy Scott
    7. Nell Ora Danielle Scott
Sp. Danny Ferris   b. 9-16-1985
6. Lois Rae Godfrey b. 3-5-1968
Sp. Rex Fackrell
4. Nellie M. Godfrey b. 1-9-1902 d. 9-21-75
Sp. Martin Anderson m. 8-25-1924
  5. Richard Rollin Anderson b. 7-28-1926 d. 2-2-1971
  Sp. Janet Steffen m. 7-2-1960
    6. Dale Martin Anderson b. 3-25-67
    6. Douglas Edward Anderson b. 2-2-71?
  5. LeRoy G. Anderson b. 9-16-1928 m. 7-6-48
  Sp. Darlene Bass b. 6-26-1932
    6. Diane Anderson b. 7-10-1949
    Sp. Percy Watson m. 6-30-1970
      7. David LeRoy Watson b. 1-7-72
      7. Daniel Martin Watson 10-15-74
    6. Tommie Anderson b. 9-13-1951
    Sp. Donnie Standiford m. 6-27-1970
    b. 9-8-53 d. 5-26-74
      7. Theresa Anderson
    6. Jerry Anderson b. 12-6-1955
4. Lillie L. Godfrey b. 7-26-1907 d.
Sp. Louis Kafader m. 11-29-1929
b. 5-2-1882 d. 2-21-1954

     5. Louis Gene Kafader b. 8-31-1936 d.
        Sp. Dorothy Ann Quector ? m. 9-1-1956
           6. Theresa May Kafader b. 7-24-1957
               Sp. N.R. Westbrook m. 7-14-1975
           6. Helen Louise Kafader b. 3-2-1961
           6. Neva Ralene Kafader b. 5-24-1965
           6. Christian Daniel Kafader 8-21-74
               Sp. Lewis C. Hatfield m. 7-1-1960
               b. 3-5-1895 d. 8-13-1963
    4. Frank H. Godfrey b. 8-14-1909 d. 10-15-09
    4. Charley T. Godfrey b. 5-10-11 d. 10-5-95
3. William Stanley b. 6-14-1876 d.
   Sp. Olive Harvey
    4. Edward William Stanley b. 9-3-1916
    4. Alvin Wayne Stanley d. at 16
    4. Dorothy Stanley b. 8-6-1920
      Sp. Roy LaLocke
      (Phyllis Katherine LaLocke b. 11-10-42 by first wife)
        5. Sally Locke b. 1-13-47
          Sp. Mike Hobkirk
           6. John Mike Hobkirk b. 8-9-57
           6. Janet Marie Hobkirk b. 8-18-68
        5. Donna Lorraine Locke b. 8-5-48
          Sp. Sheldon Louis Theouralt (sp)
           6. Linda Marie Theouralt b. 9-4-74
        5. Sandra Lee (La) Locke b. 3-7-50
          Sp. Roger Wayne Merrifield
           6. Kenneth Ray (Roy) Merrifield b. 2-18-71
        5. Diana Elizabeth Locke b. 5-1-51
        5. James B. Locke b. 8-26-52
          Sp. Janet N. ? Hemil
           6. Cristen Marie Locke b. 1-13-74
           6. Michael James Locke b. 6-1-75
        5. Linda May Locke b. 3-26-55
          Sp. Douglas Dwight Moore
           6. Douglas Dwight Moore, Jr. b. 7-14-75
        5. Robert Wayne Locke b. 5-24-57
        5. Nancy Raeline Locke b. 10-8-60
    4. Harvey Lester Stanley b. 5-3-26 d. 6-25-69
      Sp. Mary Young b. 2-4-34 m. 9-14-52
        5. William Lester Stanley b. 7-21-1953
          d. 10-19-66

5. Cheryl Lynette Stanley b. 10-11-54
5. Harvey Laurence Stanley b. 8-27-56
3. Rosa Bell Stanley b. 10-12-1878 d. 7-23-1965
Sp. Erasmus Ralph Day b. 6-15-1868 m. 9-5-1900
4. Ruby Elizabeth Day b. 2-8-1903
Sp. Carroll L. Gilmour m. 4-16-1925
(b. 2-3-1902 d. 5-4-1968)
5. Patricia Ann Gilmour b. 4-29-1932
Sp. Alan DeWitt Button
6. Sara Button b. 12-26-57
6. Jennifer Button b. 3-14-60
6. Adam Button b. 10-10-63
5. Carol Elizabeth Gilmour b. 7-10-1934
Sp. Michael Craig
6. Steven Michael Craig b. 4-29-58
4. Gerald Erasmus Day b. 2-8-1905 d. 5-2-72
Sp. Naomi Hemphill m. 12-1927
5. Geraldine Day b. 1-17-1933
Sp. Russ Williams m. 3-3-56
6. Curt Williams b. 11-58
6. Roxanna Williams b. 12-31-59
5. Kenton Stanley Day b. 6-6-36
Sp. #1
6. Debbie Day b. 2-2-55
6. Loretta Day b. 12-19-57
Sp. #2
3. Nancy Jane Stanley b. 3-21-1881 d. 5-12-1884
3. George Stanley b. 9-4-1883 d. 10-13-1921
Sp. Irene ———-
4. Roselle Stanley
4. Edna Stanley
4. Grace Stanley
3. Frank L. Stanley b. 6-1-1885 d. 11-1-1887
2. Sp. Charley Cox (Rachel's 2nd husband)
2. Joseph Louis Mendell b. 6-13-1858 d. 2-18-1926
2. John Mendell
2. Thomas Mendell b. 10-4-1860 d. 5-18-1895
2. William Henry Mendell b. 4-13-1871 d. 10-29-1944
Sp. Lillie Thom(p)son m. 10-27-1910
(b. 10-29-1885 d. 5-16-1944)

3. Charles Mendell b. 7-15-1911
    Sp. Billie ————-
3. Gail (sp) Mendell b. 7-21-1912
    Sp. Resita Alvarez
    4. Robert Mendell b. 12-26-1949
        Sp. Debbie Smith
        5. Robert Gail Mendell
    4. Alice Mendell b. 6-25-1951
    4. James Mendell b. 2-14-1953
3. Nancy Mendell b. 8-4-1914
    Sp. Lawrence Milton Shell b. 5-11-10 m. 8-10-31
    4. Nancy Lee Shell b. 6-6-1932
        Sp. Neil Burrell b. 3-21-32 m. 9-7-51
        5. Vincent Randolph Burrell b. 4-12-53
            Sp. Arlene ————-
            6. Christy Lynn Burrell 9-28-72
            6. Sara Ann Burrell b. 7-26-74
    4. Lawrence Ronald Shell b. 10-18-1933
    4. Milton Lloyd Shell b. 12-4-1935
        Sp. Susan Roberta (Lammer ?)
        5. Mark Brian Shell b. 2-19-1958
        Sp. Wanda Sue ————
    4. Karen Darlene Shell b. 9-14-1940
3. Jessie Mendell b. 5-5-1916.
3. Rachel Gayle Mendell b. 5-29-1918.
2. Narcissus Mendell

WOOD FAMILY GENEALOGY CHART

1. Wood, David Madison b. 1759 d. 9-23-1821 m. 4-8-1784.
   Sp. Johnson, Freelove Mrs. b. 4-8-1768 d. 3-17-1841.
   2. Wood, Rufus b. 12-1783 d. 8-16-1826 m. 1820.
      Sp. Catherine ———
   2. Wood, Thomas b. 1785 d.
   2. Wood, Sarah b. 1788 d. post 1855 m.
      Sp. Foster, Ira
   2. Wood, David, Jr. b. 1790 d. 5-11-1861
      Sp. Esther ———-
      3. Wood, Mary A. b. 1815
         Sp. Weller
      3. Wood, Mercy A. b. 1815
         Sp. Polly ———-
   2. Wood, Madison M. b. 1792 d. 3-8-1863 m.
      Sp. Elizabeth ——— d. 1857.
   2. Wood, Hannah b. 1793-5 d. m. ante 1820.
      Sp. Hathaway, Luther
   2. Wood, Barnabus b. 1795-6 d. m. 1830.
      Sp. Elizabeth ———
   2. Wood, Russell b. 1797-8 d. m.
      Sp. Freelove ———-
      3. Wood, Madison M.
   2. Wood, Betsy b. 1803 d. m. ca 1820.
      Sp. Sturdevant, Harvey
      3. Sturdevant, Giles b. 1827.
      3. Sturdevant, Ira S. b. 1829.
      3. Sturdevant, Sarah I. b. 1831.
      3. Sturdevant, Alma b. 1832.
      3. Sturdevant, Sophiah b. 1834.
      3. Sturdevant, Judson C. b. 1836.
      3. Sturdevant, Henry M. b. 1838.

3. Sturdevant, David N. b. 1839.

3. Sturdevant, George W. b. 1841.

3. Sturdevant, James M. b. 1843.

3. Sturdevant, Joseph L. b. 1845.

2. Wood, William b. 1804 d. 5-7-1861 m. ca 1825.

Sp. Johnson, Mahala b. 1810 d. 6-20-1859.

   3. Wood, Cordelia b. 6-22-1826 d. 3-31-1909.

   Sp. Bone, George A. W. (Capt) m. 7-30-1859

   3. Wood, John G. b. 1830. d. 4-27-1864 m. 4-16-1855.

   Sp. Britton, Harriet b. 1840 d. 5-14-1864.

      4. Wood, David William b. 5-8-1857.

      Sp. Michaut, Marie Appoline b. 11-11-1869 d. 4-12-1951

      4. Wood, John G. Jr. b. 10-8-1859.

   3. Wood, Marian b. 1834 d. 1904 m. 5-27-1855.

   Sp. (1) Brooks, Warren

      4. Brooks, Laore (Laura) m. 1-15-1872

      Sp. Hatch, Marcelan Watson

      4. Brooks, Luella

      Sp. Wilton, ————-

      Sp. (2) Rollette, Antoine m. 1-14-1865

      4. Rollette, Eliza b. 1870 d. 12-25-1945.

      Sp. Burnham, Warren Joseph d. 1939.

         5. Burnham, William Warren b. 11-28-1889d. 11-25-1952.

         Sp. Lawson, Beth S. d. 1935.

            6. Burnham, Thayer

            6. Burnham, William Leonard b. 7-8-1921

            Sp. ————, Norma Louise b. 5-4-1923

               7. Burnham, Beth Anne b. 7-25-1946.

               Sp. Olson, Bernard

                  8. Olson, Shawn Douglas b. 4-7-1969.

               7. Burnham, Sue Lynn b. 11-12-1948.

               Sp. Theno, Daniel (Senator)

                  8. Theno, Scott b. 4-4-1975

                  8. Theno, Tad b. 5-23-1977.

               7. Burnham, Mary Jo b. 2-6-1953.

               Sp. Husset, Bradford

                  8. Husset, Tarajo b. 3-13-1975.

                  8. Husset, Adam b. 2-14-1978.

                  8. Husset, Jesse b. 3-31-1982.

               7. Burnham, William Craig b. 5-23-1955.

               Sp. Showalter, Carol

       7. Burnham, Tami Lisa b. 6-28-1961
         Sp. Lundmark, Keith
      6. Burnham, Natalie
        Sp. Eberly, ————-
      6. Burnham, Elizabeth
        Sp. Nicoll, ————
      6. Burnham, Barbara
        Sp. Blanchette, ————-
    5. Burnham, Bertram Worth b. 3-16-1893
     Sp. Calkins, Jenny
       6. Burnham, Bernie (Olson) b. 12-2-1913
        (Bernie Burnham changed his name to Olson.)
          7. Olson (Burnham), Sherrie b. 3-30-1947.
           Sp. Marchinson, ————-
          7. Olson (Burnham), Gloria b. 11-24-1953.
           Sp. Garzo, ————-
          7. Olson (Burnham), JoAnne b. 8-13-1958.
       6. Burnham, Laddie (Olson) b. 12-28-1915.
        (Laddie Burnham changed his name to Olson.)
          7. Olson (Burnham), Ferdie James b. 1-24-1936
          7. Olson (Burnham), Colleen b. 5-5-1937
           Sp. Murphy, ————-
          7. Olson (Burnham), Larry b. 4-4-1938.
          7. Olson (Burnham), Cholie b. 1-4-1949.
           Sp. Shackley, ————-
          7. Olson (Burnham), Debbie b. 10-20-1953.
           Falkowski (sp), ————-
3. Wood, Amanda Mariea b. 1-26-1835 d.10-14-1924.
   Sp. Long, Edward John m. 1-3-1857.
                          b. 12-18-1827 d. 12-6-1905.
   4. Long, Marshall William b. 3-3-1859 d. 10-15-1934.
    Sp. Welton, Elizabeth Ann
      5. Long, Flora M. b. 5-16-1881 m. 6-22-1897
        Sp. Castner, Charles
      5. Long, Nellie Ethel b. 3-1-1883 d. 7-6-1946.
        Sp. Bartlett, Lorne Levi m. 1905.
      5. Long, Kathryn b. 6-30-1884.
        Sp. Cole, Lowell
      5. Long, Wayne William b. 6-14-1890 d. 11-15-1946
        Sp. Long, Leona A. m. 6-5-1912.
      5. Long, Phoebe Annabella b. 1-15-1894
        Sp. (1) Chester Faust (2) Alfred Uhl.

4. Long, Robert Henry b. 9-4-1861 d.6-20-1950.
   Sp. Jones, Mary Eva b. 4-4-1864 d. 3-11-1932.
   m. 10-15-1882
   5. Long, Robert Edward b. 6-5-1883 d. 3-3-1930
      Sp. Minot, Mabel
   5. Long, Samuel Bertrand b. 8-12-1885 d. 8-21-1973.
      Sp. Robinson, Clara J. m. 6-23-1915.
   5. Long, Leona Amanda b. 12-2-1887
      Sp. Long, Wayne William (cousin) m. 6-5-1912
   5. Long, Florence Cordelia b. 11-1-1889 d. 11-24-1978.
      Sp. Howe, Martin C. m. 7-3-1913.
   5. Long, Mae Gladys b. 6-3-1891
      Sp. (1) Guy Hankins (2) R.A. Cox.
   5. Long, Clara Christina b. 7-10-1893 d. 8-8-1981.
      Sp. McDonough, Thomas m. 3-1-1911.
   5. Long, Vern Whitney b. 2-6-1896.
      Sp. Fry, Lena L. m. 12-13-1917.
   5. Long, Baby b. d. 1899.
   5. Long, Vera Adell b. 2-12-1902 d. 12-10-1980.
      Sp. Fry, Oscar B. m. 7-15-1920.
4. Long, Ida Victoria b. 3-21-1863 d. 12-10-1943.
   Sp. Black, Peter J. b. 1856 d. 4-11-1908
   m. 3-7-1883.
   5. Black, Gerald b. 1884.
   5. Black, Laura Ozeda b. 1885 d.1969.
      Sp. McFadden, Robert
   5. Black, LaVerne Nelson b. 1887 d.1938
   5. Black, Marcena b. 1888 d. 1915.
      Sp. Worrell, ———
   5. Black, Byron Bayard b. 1890 d. 10-6-1960.
   5. Black, Buelah A. b. 7-4-1897 d. 1980.
      Sp. Shadbolt, Horace A.
   5. Black, Donald Robert b. 11-11-1906
4. Long, Sarah Helene b. 4-18-1886 d. 10-17-1941.
   Sp. Jones, Samuel Eugene m. 12-31-1882.
   b. 6-14-1853 d. 1-10-1937.
   5. Jones, Laura Adell b. 10-1-1883 d. 2-20-1968.
      Sp. (1) Charles F. Adams (2) Volkert V. Smith.
   5. Jones, Ida Belle b. 1-12-1885 d. 2-19-1887.
   5. Jones, Roy Francis b. 5-11-1888 d. 4-27-1889.

4. Long, Edna Elnora b. 2-7-1880 d.12-20-1943.
   Sp. Wood, Frank Elliot m. 11-21-1901
                             b. 12-6-1866 d. 6-25-1958.
   5. Wood, Bruce George b. 12-20-1902 d. 1-27-1984.
      Sp. Schott, Marguerite
      6. Wood, Leslie August b. 8-16-1939/40.
         Sp. Masseth, Beverly Jean b. 6-27-1941.
         7. Wood, Rusty Joseph b. 2-28-1961.
         7. Wood, Ronald Bruce b. 4-7-1962.
         7. Wood, Jody Marie b. 10-2-1963.
         7. Wood, Randy August b. 8-22-1966.
         7. Wood, Anthony Joseph b. 5-5-1981.
      6. Wood, Sandra Elthea b. 9-17-1942.
         Sp. Green, Leo Tracy b. 1-17-1942 m. 9-17-1960.
         7. Green, Margaret Lorena b. 10-27-1962.
         7. Green, Cyndy Louella b. 10-20-1964.
            Sp. Davenport, Tony Lee m. 4-4-1984.
         7. Green, Tracy Leona b. 1-1-1968.
         7. Green, William Lee b. 11-24-1970.
      Sp. (2) Lindsay, Kathleen.
   5. Wood, Marshal Ney b. 2-7-1904 d. 9-24-43.
      Sp. Pilgeram, Marie Ann b. 12-23-1907.
                              m. 11-22-1930 d. 12-18-1991.
      6. Wood, Oren Marshall b. 4-22-1933.
         Sp. Hisae Miyoshi m. 8-9-1957.
         7. Wood, Marshal Ray b. 2-2-1963 d. 9-20-1984.
      6. Wood, Lorraine Marie b. 1935.
         Sp. Hankins, Roy Raymond
         7. Hankins, Wendy
            Sp. Hallas, ———
         7. Hankins, Christy
            Sp. Olson, ———-
         7. Hankins, Valerie
            Sp. Parsons, ———
   5. Wood, Warren Edward b. 4-6-1906 d. 1-28-1984.
      Sp. (1) Minnie Sewell (2) ? (3) Josie Morgan.
   5. Wood, Victor Marion b. 5-28-1907 d. 1986.
      Sp. (1) Joan Moore (2) Mabel Ruth Sharpe
3. Wood, Dau b. 1836 d. young
3. Wood, George M. b. 1840/1 d. 7-14-1892.
   Sp. Faust, Lorinda b. 1846 m. 5-22-1864 d. 1900.

4. Wood, Frank Elliot b. 12-6-1866 d. 6-25-1958.
   Sp. Long, Edna Elnora (See page 191 for issue)
4. Wood, Calvin Arthur b. 5-20-1867 d. 12-2-1957.
   Sp. Smith, Delilah b. 1847 d. 1-4-1945.
     5. Wood, Ralph b. 2-28-1896 d. 1954
       Sp. Phillips, Doris m. 1951.
     5. Wood, Addie b. 11-17-1897 d.
       Sp. (1) Garr, John
         6. Garr, Helen b. d. 1984
           Sp. Karrels, Henry
         6. Garr, Florence
           Sp. Baughman, Fred
             7. Baughman, Donald
             7. Baughman, Joyce
             7. Baughman, Fred
     5. Wood, Elsie b. 3-23-1900 d. 1983.
       Sp. Alexander, Earl
         6. Alexander, Dorothy
           Sp. Ashley, Maurice
             7. Ashley, Glenda
         6. Alexander, Marietta
           Sp. (1) Garrett (2) Kimbal
             7. ?, Donald
             7. ?, Sherry
             7. ?, Douglas
             7. ?, Susan
         6. Alexander, Bonnie
           Sp. Kiel. Maurice (2 children)
         6. Alexander, Glen
           Sp. ———, Evelyn
             7. Alexander, Glendolyn
     5. Wood, Alta b. 12-6-1904
       Sp. (1) ?
       Sp. (2) Sawyer, William
         6. ?, Robert
           Sp. ———, Carolyn
     5. Wood, Elvina b. 1-3-1902.
       Sp. Farrel, Lew
         6. Farrel, Opal
           Sp. Jacobson, Jake
             7. Jacobson, Sandy
             7. Jacobson, Danny
             7. Jacobson, Jack

7. Jacobson, Roy
7. Jacobson, Mary
7. Jacobson, Patty-Jo
6. Farrel, Doris
Sp. Titus, Regie
7. Titus, Andre
7. Titus, Laurinda
6. Farrel, Carl
6. Farrel, Grant
Sp. ?, Elizabeth, No issue
5. Wood, Wesley b. 10-28-1906.
Sp. ?, Frances
6. Wood, Jeannette
Sp. Jaordan, Loran
7. Jaordan, Eileen
7. Jaordan, Linda
7. Jaordan, Lawrence
6. Wood, Charlotte
Sp. Backus, Titus
7. Backus, Sandy
7. Backus, Chris
7. Backus, Don
7. Backus, Ellen
6. Wood, Theresa
Sp. Falzerano, James
7. Falzerano, Douglas
7. Falzerano, Jerry
7. Falzerano, Warren
7. Falzerano, Laura
7. Falzerano, Linda
6. Wood, Willard
Sp. ?, Charlotte
7. Wood, Carrie
7. Wood, Marilyn
7. Wood, Mike
7. Wood, Cindy
7. Wood, Wayne
7. Wood, Sherry
5. Wood, Keith b. 2-14-1910 (twin)
Sp. ?, Florence
6. Wood, Calvin
Sp. ?, Patricia
7. Wood, Christopher

        7. Wood, James
      6. Wood, Stanley
      Sp. ?, Shirley (no issue)
      6. Wood, Cathy
      Sp. Kling, Edward
         7. Kling, Jason
         7. Kling, Kimberly
   5. Wood, Kenneth b. 2-14-1910 (twin)
   Sp. ?, Mable
      6. Wood, Gilbert
      Sp. ?, Kathy
         7. Wood, Travis
         7. Wood, Jane
         7. Wood, Clinton
      6. Wood, Norman
      Sp. ?, Cleo, (no issue)
      6. Wood, Marjorie
      Sp. Adams, Robert
         7. Adams, Jerry Duane
         7. Adams, Ronnie
         7. Adams, Donnie
   5. Wood, Arthur b. 5-1912
   Sp. ?, Doris
      6. Wood, Rose
      Sp. ? James
         7. ?, Jamie
         7. ?, David
      6. Wood, Eleanor
      Sp. Keller, Ben
         7. Keller, James
         7. Keller, William
      6. Wood, Marsha
      Sp. ?, Robert
         7. ?, David
         7. ?, Steven
         7. ?, Mark
      6. Wood, Susan
      Sp. ?, John
         7. ?, Shawn
         7. ?, Carrie
      6. Wood, Jo-Ellen
      Sp. ?, George
         7. ?, Brian

       7. ?, Kimberly
    6. Wood, Carol dean
       Sp. ?, Daniel, (no issue)
    6. Wood, Dixie
       Sp. ?, William
       7. ?, Nell
       7. ?, William, Jr.

4. Wood, Otho Charles b. 6-10-1873 d. 8-27-1947
  Sp. Flaugher, Mattie b. 9-14-1878 m. 4-27-1896
                   d. 1934
    5. Wood, George Clifford b. 3-22-1904 d. 6-20-1967.
       Sp. Caldwell, Uintah
       6. Wood, Donald
          Sp. Wood, Doris
       6. Wood, Violet Kathleen (Georgie). 11-6-1925
          Sp. Ottarson, Doyle
          7. Ottarson, Wynn
             Sp. Rodda, William
          7. Rodda, James Guy
       6. Wood, Donna Lavine b. 9-20-1927 d. 7-27-1929
       6. Wood, Geraldine Marie b. 9-29-1933 d.
          Sp. Marsters, Harold
       Sp. Painter, Bernice
       6. Wood, Dale
       6. Wood, Bobby d. 1997
       6. Wood, Judy d. 1997
          Sp. ?, Sylvia
    5. Wood, Elizabeth Maxine (Tendering) b. 11-1-1919.
       Sp. Godfrey, LeRoy E.
       (See Godfrey Family Chart)
       Sp. Edwards, William T.
       (See Edwards Family Chart)

4. Wood, Arden R. b. 8-28-1875 d. 10-3-1955.
  Sp. Porter, Daisy m. 12-5-1900.
    5. Wood, May
       Sp. DuBois, ———-
       6. DuBois, daughter b. 7-14-1928 d. 9-1-1931.
  Sp. Bruener, Clara Blood b. 7-3-1887 d. 10-13-1947.
                m. 5-26-1902
    5. Wood, Wallace Trevette b. 3-28-1906 d. 1970.
       Sp. Frieze, Lillian m. 6-15-1939
       Sp. Evans, Evelyn m. 9-20-1958.

5. Wood, Iva M. b. 5-18-1908 d. 6-10-1925
   Sp. Turner, Francis.
5. Wood, Doris Angela b. 5-16-1909 d. 7-6-1980.
   Sp. Wood, George C. m. 9-8-1923 and 1-6-1925.
   (See Wood, George Clifford above)
   Sp. Benner, Warren "Ike" m. 12-20-1938.
    6. Benner, Angela.
     Sp. Benner, William.
   Sp. Morgan, J.R.
5. Wood, Herbert Lincoln b. 2-12-1911 d. 8-18-1994.
   Sp. Wheeler, Marcella F. b. 12-10-1917
             m. 5-16-1933
    6. Wood, Connie Joy b. 12-8-1935 m. 3-2-1953.
    Sp. Clark, Steve
     7. Clark, Donald Eugene b. 3-29-1954.
      Sp. Chmielowiez, Kazimiera m. 8-6-1976.
       8. Clark, Misty Lynn b. 9-1-1977.
       8. Clark, Wendy Leigh b. 2-16-1980.
       8. Clark, Lacey Rene b. 11-1-1984.
       8. Clark, Casey Ray b. 2-28-1986.
     7. Clark, Jerry DeWayne b. 11-7-1955.
      Sp. Faulkner, Linda Iren m. 12-21-1974
       8. Clark, Brandon DeWayne b. 7-28-1976.
       8. Clark, April Dene b. 8-30-1977.
        9. Clark, Shelby Lynn b. 9-30-1995.
       8. Clark, Cody James b. 10-28-1980.
     7. Clark, Kelly Lee b. 11-4-1959.
      Sp. Gee, Cynthia Anne m. 7-19-1980
       8. Clark, Ronnie Lee b. 12-17-1984.
       8. Clark, Ryan James b. 4-24-1987.
     7. Clark, Tammy Kay b. 3-12-1961.
      Sp. Foster, Brad m. 6-25-1982
       8. Foster, Kyle Jay b. 10-12-1983.
        Sp. Sherlock, James m. 6-28-1986
       8. Sherlock, Cory Tyler b. 9-4-1986.
    6. Wood, Ronald Herbert b. 6-13-1938 d. 2-3-1971.
    Sp. Gilbert, Sheila b. 5-28-1937.
          m. 12-29-1963.
    6. Wood, Alton Francis b. 10-3-1939.
    Sp. Merrell, Patricia m. 12-29-1963.
     7. Wood, Shaun Kevin b. 10-11-1964
      Sp. Wentzel, Patricia m. 6-25-1988.
       8. Wood, Travis Alton b. 12-24-1987

      8. Wood, Josh Kevin b. 4-19-1991.
      8. Wood, Tyler Louis b. 10-6-1992.
    7. Wood, Shane Lincoln b. 2-2-1968.
    Sp. Foster, Jolie m. 12-28-1991.
      8. Wood, Derek Lincoln b. 2-3-1994.
      8. Wood, Shanea Rene b. 8-28-1996.
5. Sp. Vernon, Alta Fay b. 2-6-1920 m. 8-16-1941.
5. Wood, Neil Robert b. 4-29-1914 d. 9-21-1991.
Sp. Johnston, Nellie Maude
Sp. King, Wilma
Sp. Murphy, Gladys.
5. Wood, Emmett Merion b. 9-21-1915 d. 3-16-1985.
Sp. Layton, Viola L. b. 6-2-1918 m. 6-5-1939.
5. Wood, Lucille Wilma b. 3-2-1921 m. 9-3-1936.
Sp. Feehan, James Francis d. 11-27-1976.
  6. Feehan, Hugh Joseph b. 5-21-1937 d. 1937.
  6. Feehan, Carol Ann b. 4-20-1940
  Sp. Ask, Richard
    7. Ask, Jerry
    7. Ask, Shannon
    7. Ask, Jennifer
  Sp. Hughes, Charles A. d. 1969.
  Sp. Spear, William
  Sp. Palmer, Clyde
5. Wood, George Wentworth b. 4-29-1922 (twin) d. 3-29-1995.
Sp. Randall, Reda
  6. Wood, Diana
  6. Wood, Cecil
5. Wood, Gene Oliver b. 4-29-1922 (twin)
Sp. Stewart, Dorothy Lucille
  6. Wood, John A. b. 10-24-1947
  Sp. Simpson, Roberta A. b. 7-24-1948.
    7. Wood, Michele A. b. 6-9-1966
    Sp. Leonard, Thomas E. b. 12-24-1958.
      8. Leonard, Thomas J. b. 6-20-1992.
    7. Wood, Angela L. b. 8-20-1969.
    Sp. Study, Westley J. b. 10-23-1959.
      8. Study, John W.
    7. Wood, Barbara R. b. 12-24-1971
    Sp. Bodden, Raymond
      8. Bodden, Ashley R. b. 2-25-1991
  6. Wood, Gene Oliver, Jr. b. 12-2-1950
  Sp. Hall, Jessie D.

      7. Wood, Gene Oliver, III b. 7-23-1969.

         Sp. ?, Linda

      7. Wood, John J. b. 2-2-1977.

      7. Wood, Destiny b. 2-4-1995

         Sp. Ritter, Bonnie

      7. Wood, Kenna

   5. Wood, Viola (McGinnis) b. post 1923. (twin)
                  d. 1994.

   Sp. Teske, Ted

   5. Wood, Rose (McGinnis) b. post 1923 (twin)
                  d. 1990

   Sp. Willis, William

4. Wood, Anna b. 5-10-1877 d. 6-22-1961.

Sp. Russell, Charles

Sp. Potter, John

   5. Potter, Alice b. 6-5-1899 d. 1-??-1996

      Sp. Raskob, Peter Paul b. 10-4-1893 d. 3-14-1964.

      6. Raskob, Marie Jeannette b. 4-27-1920

         Sp. Harmon, William Douglas

         7. Harmon, Patrick William b. 5-11-1946

            Sp. Taylor, Sharon L. m. 6-2-1968.

            8. Harmon, Trevor Wade

            8. Harmon, Deena Christina

            8. Harmon, Evan Baker

         7. Harmon, Michele Marie b. 12-2-1948

            Sp. Chandler, David Truman

                    b. 11-4-1947.

                    m. 10-24-1969.

            8. Chandler, Robert David b. 6-3-1970.

            8. Chandler, Brian Scott b. 5-13-1977.

      6. Raskob, Paul b. 3-8-1924.

         Sp. Hall, Madene

      Sp. Merrill, ———-

      Sp. Leslie, ———-

         7. Leslie, Charles W.

      Sp. Tucker, ———-

   Sp. Berryman, James F. m. 11-13-1907.

      6. Berryman, Helen Christine

4. Wood, Robert I. b. 2-5-1889 d.

Sp. Moody, Charity

   5. Wood, Robert M. b.

   Sp. Jones, Helen

   6. Wood, Susan
       Sp. Writer, ————-
   6. Wood, Mary
       Sp. Barreno, ————-
5. Wood, Harriet
    Sp. Kelley, ————-

INDEX

Scrugham, James G. ... 41
Seminario, Johnnie ... 86
Seminario, Mary ... 55
Server, Ernest ... 109
Server, Maude ... 121
Shaddack, Sally ... 115
Shakespeare ... 155
Sharp, Hattie ... 121
Sharp, John C. ... 55
Sheldon Antelope Refuge ... 23, 78
Sistok, Pete ... 121
Smith, Al ... 65
Smith, Henry E. ... 55
Smith, Joseph ... 142
Smith, Mr. ... 77, 80-81
Smith, Mrs. (Cook) ... 93
Socrates ... 18, 110, 129
Spaulding, John ... 142
Stanley, Fred ... 74
Stanley, Heath ... 86
Stanley, Lucille ... 74
Stanley, Phyllis Dolores ... 74
Staples, Gene ... 94
Stearns, Edward H. ... 143
Stevens, H. B. ... 86
Steward, Bertha ... 50
Steward, Charlotte ... 50
Steward, Oscar ... 50, 153
Steward, Robert ... 50
Stewart & Kirkpatrick ... 144
Stiles, Dr. ... 45, 55
Stovall, Jesse Lee ... 77
Strief, W. T. ... 86
Strom ... 94
Strotts, Jesse ... 64
Sturgis, General ... 51-52
Swancott, Dave ... 47-48, 54
Swancott, Effie ... 54
Swanson, Ernest ... 26
Swanson, Mrs. ... 121
Sweeney, Maggie ... 108

T

T——, Dorothy ... 73
T——, Jackie ... 73

Taylor, Albert ... 148
Taylor, Fred M. ... 55
Templeton, H. T. ... 144
Tendering, Charles Eugene ... 147
Tendering, Charles Henry, Jr. ... 47, 89, 145, 147
Tendering, Charles Henry, Sr. ... 145
Tibbits, Mora ... 88-89
Tibbits, Roy ... 88
Tierney, Hallie ... 77, 121
Tierney, Ray ... 74
Tobias, Mrs. ... 90
Tommy ... 44, 47, 147
Toney, Kesner ... 107
Toney, Maxine ... 107
Turner, Iva (Wood) ... 37
Turner, Jay ... 118
Turner, Raymond ... 74
Twain, Mark ... 122, 143
Tyeryar, "Bud" ... 56

U

Unger, C. L. ... 45
Urells, Mitchell ... 64

V

Van Horn, Bess ... 121
Van Riper, Arthur ... 44
Vine, Aunt ... 41
Vinton, Ann ... 142
Vinyard, Virgil A. ... 77

W

Ward, Erma ... 131
Washoe, Jimmie ... 109
Watkins, Charley ... 118
Weilmunster, Alex ... 61
Weilmunster, Daisy ... 61
Weilmunster, Leo ... 41
Whaley, Mrs. ... 105
Wheeler, George ... 141
Wheeler, Marcella ... 77, 102
White, Ricardo ... 134
Willard, Simon ... 142
Williams, Phillip D. ... 123

LEGEND

Robert Fletcher	b. 1591/2 Skropshire, Yorkshire, England
John Heald	b. 1615 Berwick-on-Tweed
Samuel Heald	b. 9-12-1668 Mobberly, Cheshire, England